Faculty Research Performance: Lessons from the Sciences and the Social Sciences

John W. Creswell

ASHE-ERIC Higher Education Report No. 4, 1985

Prepared by

® *Clearinghouse on Higher Education*
The George Washington University

Published by

ASHE

Association for the Study of Higher Education

Jonathan D. Fife,
Series Editor

Cite as
Creswell, John W. *Faculty Research Performance: Lessons from the Sciences and the Social Sciences*. ASHE-ERIC Higher Education Report No. 4. Washington, D.C.: Association for the Study of Higher Education, 1985.

The ERIC Clearinghouse on Higher Education invites individuals to submit proposals for writing monographs for the Higher Education Report series. Proposals must include:
1. A detailed manuscript proposal of not more than five pages.
2. A 75-word summary to be used by several review committees for the initial screening and rating of each proposal.
3. A vita.
4. A writing sample.

Library of Congress Catalog Card Number 85-103507
ISSN 0884-0040
ISBN 0-913317-23-3

ERIC® **Clearinghouse on Higher Education**
The George Washington University
One Dupont Circle, Suite 630
Washington, D.C. 20036

ASHE **Association for the Study of Higher Education**
One Dupont Circle, Suite 630
Washington, D.C. 20036

This publication was partially prepared with funding from the National Institute of Education, U.S. Department of Education under contract no. 400-82-0011. The opinions expressed in this report do not necessarily reflect the positions or policies of NIE or the Department.

Executive Summary

Why some faculty produce research year after year and others do not is a "puzzle" (Cole, J. and Zuckerman 1984). Despite at least 90 studies since 1940 (Fox 1983), the measures of research performance are vague and poorly understood. Researchers do not clearly identify explanations for high research performance. The specific correlates of high performance are fraught with measurement problems, unclear causality, and unspecified predictive power. Moreover, the results from empirical studies are not translated into practical use for the resolution of such faculty issues as faculty development and faculty evaluation.

This study reviews the literature on faculty research performance. It examines the measures of performance, the explanations and specific correlates likely to influence high research performance, and the practical implications of empirical studies for faculty development and evaluation. Only *individual* faculty research is discussed; analyses of research performance by departments, colleges, and institutions are available elsewhere. Further, only "research" is examined, acknowledging that faculty engage in important service and teaching activities as well as research. Finally, this study reviews results reported about science and social science faculty as discussed primarily in the literature on sociology and the sociology of science, recognizing that faculty in the arts, humanities, and other disciplines also engage in valuable research activities.

How is research performance, especially high performance, measured?
Few writers specifically discuss alternative measures of research performance, and few identify their conception of research or that of their respondents (Finkelstein 1984). Even attempting to measure faculty performance disturbs some people who consider it unmeasurable (Yuker 1978). Still, data-based studies of science and social science faculty use three common measures: publication counts, citation counts, and peer-colleague ratings.

Publication counts, which measure the *quantity* of an individual's output, are obtained by simply counting the number of publications ("straight count") or by counting the number of publications using a weighted scale for each type of publication ("weighted count"). "Publications" often include articles published in scholarly journals and books and monographs. Publication counts may have limited accuracy because they give equal credit to poorly conceived papers appearing in badly edited journals as well as to well-written papers in quality journals (except when a "weighted" scale of quality is used). In addition, publication counts do not consider such factors as coauthorship and the length of published works.

Citation counts, which measure the *quality* of a publication and its *influence* on academic knowledge and the academic community, are obtained by counting citations reported in published indices, such as the *Science Citation Index* (SCI), the *Social Science Citation Index* (SSCI), and the *Arts and Humanities Citation Index.* Information in these indices reports the number of times an individual's publications are cited. Through the published indices, researchers can easily and objectively trace a faculty member's research record. However, citation counts may reflect fads in citing popular works and may not accurately show the precise impact of a published work. Other problems are inherent in published indices, such as citing works by the first author only.

Peer or colleague ratings, which measure the *reputation* of a scholar or researcher in the academic community (Cole, J. 1979), are obtained from questionnaires, letters, or interviews. Ratings often include an assessment of the perceived quality and visibility of an individual's work. They are widely used in evaluating faculty performance for promotion and tenure. Ratings may accurately portray performance because peers know the researcher's work and feel qualified to compare it with that of others (Pelz and Andrews 1966). However, they may also provide inadequate or false information, reflect the "halo" effect of a scholar's employing institution, and be inconsistent when made by several peers.

What explains why some faculty become high research producers (or prolific producers) and others do not?
Evidence shows that the average rate of faculty publication tends to be low and the variation in performance very high (Fox 1983). Writers explain this variation in several ways.

Productive researchers possess certain *psychological* and *individual* characteristics that are absent in less productive researchers. High producers may have "innate" scientific ability or talent, possess a "sacred spark" of motivation and desire, and have a certain type of personality or cognitive structure. Biographical studies of eminent scientists reveal hard-working people who play with ideas, recombine familiar concepts easily, and tolerate ambiguity and abstraction (Fox 1983). High producers also tend more often to be men than women, and they sustain high performance levels throughout their careers.

Productive researchers *cumulate advantages* during their careers, such as training in a prestigious graduate program, employment in a major research university, and the availability of adequate resources for research.

Productive researchers are *reinforced* in their research efforts by colleagues' citing and praising their works, and by having their works accepted for publication early in their careers. According to one author,

> *Unless a person achieves a qualitative piece of research during his first five years as a sociologist . . . it seems unlikely that he will do so during the next five years—if at any time during his career* (Lightfield 1971, p. 133).

Productive researchers are shaped and molded by the *norms of their discipline* to publish in select outlets and to engage in specific research activities. For example, in disciplines in which knowledge is highly codified and individuals agree on important questions and methods (e.g., physics), faculty publish more in journals (an abbreviated form of communication) than in books (an extended form of communication) (Gaston 1978).

What specific correlates (or factors) influence high research performance?
Researchers have tested the general explanations of high research performance using a complex set of correlates. Evidence suggests that sociological and work-environment correlates (e.g., amount of time spent on research) may explain performance more precisely than psychological correlates (e.g., I.Q.). The impact of a correlate, however, seems highly related to the type of measure (e.g., journal articles versus books) and the discipline being studied.

Still, from numerous correlate studies in the past 40 years, a profile of productive researchers has emerged. A productive researcher—

- is employed in a major university that rewards research and assigns ample time for faculty to conduct research;
- holds senior professorial rank, though performance may peak 10 years after the doctorate and again later toward the end of a career;
- spends at least one-third of time on research activities;
- began publishing early in career and received positive feedback from peers for research efforts (Cole, J. and and Cole, S. 1973); and
- maintains regular and close contact (e.g., telephone calls) with colleagues on and off campus who conduct research on similar topics.

What are the implications of the literature on research performance for faculty development, faculty evaluation, and future research?

The literature on research performance can inform faculty and academic administrators about strategies for developing faculty as researchers and for evaluating faculty performance. Traditional literature on *faculty development* suggests that faculty can develop as researchers by taking sabbatical leaves, attending professional meetings, and securing funds for projects. The correlate studies present additional strategies. Graduate students can select outstanding graduate programs for their training. Faculty can begin publishing soon after graduation, maintain a continuous level of research throughout their career, keep in continuous contact with other scholars working on similar projects, and establish a preference for and time for research in their work schedule. Administrators and faculty committees can reinforce and stimulate faculty research by employing graduates of quality programs, promoting and tenuring faculty who are productive researchers, providing faculty with time and resources to conduct studies, and creating an attitude and atmosphere in a department or a college that values research.

In the *faculty-evaluation process,* faculty and personnel committees should recognize that research performance varies by discipline and the stage of a faculty career and that multiple measures of research performance should be used in assessing research effort. Further, when publication counts are used, they can be supplemented by a qualitative index of publications.

Future research studies should include (a) using criterion measures in addition to publications, citations, and ratings (e.g., number of patents); (b) tests of explanations of performance based on an interdisciplinary approach; (c) tests of models in which academic rank, institution, discipline, and career age are held constant so that substantive work-environment correlates can be examined; and (d) continued efforts to examine the practical implications of the literature on research performance.

ADVISORY BOARD

CONSULTING EDITORS

Robert Atwell
President
American Council on Education

Robert Cope
Professor of Higher Education
University of Washington

Robert L. Craig
Former Vice President, Government Affairs
American Society for Training and Development, Inc.

John W. Creswell
Associate Professor
Department of Educational Administration
University of Nebraska

Mary F. Fox
Associate Professor
Center for Research on Social Organization
University of Michigan

W. Lee Hansen
Professor
Department of Economics
University of Wisconsin

David Kaser
Professor
School of Library and Information Science
Indiana University

George Keller
Senior Vice President
Barton-Gillet Company

David W. Leslie
Professor and Chair
Department of Educational Leadership
The Florida State University

Ernest A. Lynton
Commonwealth Professor and Senior Associate
Center for the Study of Policy and the Public Interest
University of Massachusetts

Gerald W. McLaughlin
Institutional Research and Planning Analysis
Virginia Polytechnic Institute and State University

Theodore J. Marchese
Vice President
American Association for Higher Education

L. Jackson Newell
Professor and Dean
University of Utah

Harold Orlans
Office of Programs and Policy
United States Civil Rights Commission

Lois S. Peters
Center for Science and Technology Policy
New York University

John M. Peterson
Director, Technology Planning
The B. F. Goodrich Company

Richard H. Quay
Social Science Librarian
Miami University

John E. Stecklein
Professor of Educational Psychology
University of Minnesota

James H. Werntz, Jr.
Vice Chancellor for Academic Affairs
University of North Carolina

Donald Williams
Professor of Higher Education
University of Washington

CONTENTS

Foreword	**xv**
Acknowledgments	**xvii**
Dedication	**xix**
Introduction	**1**
Background	2
Purpose and Scope of Study	3
Measures of Faculty Research Performance	**7**
Publication Counts	8
Citation Counts	11
Ratings of Performance	13
Summary	14
Conceptual Explanations of Research Performance	**15**
Psychological-Individual Explanations	16
Cumulative Advantage	18
Reinforcement	19
Disciplinary Norms	21
Summary	25
Correlates of Research Performance	**27**
Intelligence Test Scores	29
Motivation	29
Personality Characteristics	30
Stress	31
Age	31
Gender	33
Prestige of Doctoral Program and Mentoring	35
Prestige of Employing Institution	36
Resources and Assignment	37
Colleagues	38
Academic Rank and Tenure	39
Early Productivity	40
Preference for Research	41
Disciplinary Differences	42
Summary and General Observations	43
Implications for Practice and Future Research	**45**
Faculty Research Development	45
Faculty Evaluation and Research Productivity	51
Research Agendas	55
Summary	56
References	**59**
Index	**69**

FOREWORD

In the next decade, the percentage of tenured faculty at colleges and universities will rise, to include perhaps more than 75 percent of all available positions. Many of these tenured slots are already held by distinguished professors who achieved their senior rank at a relatively young age and who will remain productive for at least another decade. What can administrators do to improve or maintain scholarly productivity during the different phases of a professional career? What is known about productive and non-productive performers? What steps can an institution or department take to create, enhance, and promote productivity?

These are the issues addressed in this ASHE-ERIC report, the fourth in the 1985 series. Although teaching is and will remain the primary function for the majority of all faculty, the subject of research performance will have a marked influence in determining the face of academe tomorrow.

When judgments are made regarding a faculty member's worth to an institution, research or scholarly performance and productivity will play an increasingly important role. An institution whose search committees and tenure review committees best judge tomorrow's high producers will prosper more easily than others. Just as important, the institution that can create an atmosphere that encourages faculty members to remain productive throughout their careers will measurably improve their stature in the professional community. As this report shows, the ability to attract top-flight talent will be wasted if the school environment is not conducive to high performance. High research performance is already admired and desired throughout the institutional structure. Scholarly productivity enhances a faculty member's teaching ability by providing better insight to the discipline and contributing to the latest developments. Presidents and trustees value productivity for the visibility and reputation it indirectly earns for the institution. Administrators and deans admire productivity for the creative, stimulating forces it brings into the collegial atmosphere. The academic community smiles upon scholarly work because it advances knowledge.

Perhaps no one benefits more from publishing than the researchers themselves. The objective display of one's work in a critical atmosphere can lead to sharper scholars, more adept teachers, and better communicators. If nothing else, an author receives a great boost of self-confidence at seeing his or her work published. At research-oriented institutions, 'publish or perish' is more than a slogan; it is the wheel about which the success of an institution, and each individual in it, revolves.

Although the importance of high research performance is understood, what is not so readily accepted is the definitive, preferred method of gauging productivity. Which is more useful in establishing the total output of a faculty member—publication counts or citations? Which is the more important contribution within a discipline—a book or a journal article? What should be weighed more heavily in determining a scholar's value—peer reviews or professional reputation? How should publications data be collected—self-reporting or surveys of bibliographies and databases? In attempting to unravel the answers to these and other questions, John Creswell, associate professor of education at the University of Nebraska, analyzes the research findings on faculty productivity and examines the methodology of evaluating faculty research performance. He explores the common factors among high research performers to identify the causes for the wide variance in scholarly performance among faculty members.

The significance of this ASHE-ERIC report is its emphasis of the crucial role that the institutional environment plays in allowing those so inclined to be productive. Developing the proper atmosphere on a campus is not beholden to financial considerations or extensive studies. Any institution is able to schedule research time into each member's schedule, to offer positive reinforcement informally at faculty meetings or formally with a publications party, to encourage creative and curious minds to follow their ideas with research. Productivity cannot be artificially created by an institution. But an oppressive climate will snuff out the spark of productivity every time. This is the administrative challenge for tomorrow.

Jonathan D. Fife
Series Editor
Professor and Director
ERIC Clearinghouse on Higher Education
The George Washington University

ACKNOWLEDGMENTS

For suggestions about the shape and content of this report and for guidance on many problems of editing, I owe much to Dr. Michael Barnes, Dr. Robert Patterson, and Patricia Murphy of the University of Nebraska-Lincoln; Dr. Nancy Langston and Mary Megel of the University of Nebraska College of Nursing; Dr. John Braxton of Northeastern Illinois University; and Dr. Clifton Conrad of the University of Arizona. During the summer of 1984, the University of Nebraska-Lincoln provided necessary time and resources for work on this manuscript through a Maude Hammon Fling Summer Research Fellowship.

I also owe much to my family, Karen, David, and Johanna, who provided the necessary support, encouragement, and time away from the family to see this report to its completion.

John W. Creswell
Lincoln, Nebraska
June 1985

DEDICATION

This research report is dedicated to Carolbel C. Peters, my
sister, who passed away during the preparation of this
manuscript. Though her voice will no longer be heard
praising high performance, the example of her own short,
productive life will live on.

INTRODUCTION

Most college and university professors in the United States do not think of themselves as researchers. Faculty describe themselves primarily as teachers and engage mainly in teaching (Fulton and Trow 1974). Over half of American professors have published nothing or very little (Ladd 1979). Still, research is a valued activity in postsecondary education. Whether or not faculty themselves engage in research, they seem to believe that a most important activity for an academic is the performance of significant research (Ladd 1979). And research is no longer the prerogative of doctorate-granting institutions and major universities; state colleges and liberal arts schools have begun to stress research, publications, and involvement in professional societies (Seldin 1984b).

Several compelling reasons exist for faculty to engage in research. Faculty research brings state, regional, and national visibility to academic institutions. It becomes a means whereby an institution can establish a reputation for outstanding faculty and demonstrate achievement and progress to the public (Meisinger, Purves, and Schmidtlein 1975). Faculty research lends an element of objectivity to the promotion and tenure processes when it can be codified and included on a vita so that peers can review it easily (Ladd 1979). Research also contributes to public knowledge by developing a rational consensus in fields of study with burgeoning scholarly and technical journals and books (Carnegie Council on Policy Studies in Higher Education 1980; Ziman 1968).

The value of research on college and university campuses is understood by those working on the campuses. Less clear is how faculty *perform* at research. For example, few writers specifically discuss alternative measures of research performance, and few identify their conception of research or that of their respondents (Finkelstein 1984). Even attempting to measure faculty performance disturbs some who consider it unmeasurable (Yuker 1978). And yet, writers studying research performance use common criterion measures. Faculty personnel committees make judgments about a candidate's credentials based on select measures.

Faculty vary in their research performance levels (Allison 1980). Why some faculty become major research producers year after year and others do not is a "puzzle"

Most college and university professors in the United States do not think of themselves as researchers.

(Cole, J. and Zuckerman 1984). Writings in sociology, psychology, and social psychology provide tentative solutions to the "puzzle." Specific factors—correlates—associated with high productivity have been widely discussed since 1940 in the literature on the sociology of science. Jonathan Cole and Zuckerman (1984) cited 40 studies published since 1975. Fox (1983) summarized approximately 90 studies. From these works and others, researchers can assemble a composite picture of productive research faculty.

That picture, though, is an abstract image. Important practical implications seem apparent from the studies, especially for faculty development and evaluation, but researchers infrequently discuss them. This may be due to the dominance of theoretical, data-based studies in the literature. It may also be a commentary on the current state of the art of research. Regardless of the reason, a need exists to bridge the empirical literature on research performance and the applied literature on faculty.

Background
Early studies examining faculty research performance began in the 1940s and 1950s when writers first studied "faculty" in higher education. Logan Wilson's (1942) sociological study, *The Academic Man,* is a good case in point. In a comprehensive study of many aspects of academic life, Wilson touched on research productivity in a review of how academics spent their time. He found teaching to be the primary occupation of faculty; research was of little importance, especially in performance appraisals. Wilson's observations supported the conclusion that the person who published research, or creative or interpretative writing, was not promoted as rapidly as the person who confined his or her activities to classroom teaching.

In another study of faculty approximately 15 years later, Lazarsfeld and Thielens (1958) examined social scientists who were high producers. High research producers—individuals who published dissertations, papers, and books and who read papers at professional meetings—were officers in professional organizations, moved from institution to institution, and often came from high socioeconomic families.

In the late 1950s, practical reasons developed for the study of faculty in higher education. In the post-sputnik era, researchers collaborated with others in federally and privately funded research laboratories. Policymakers became concerned about maximum research performance in the laboratories and the effects of the research environment on scientific performance (Kaplan 1964). Funded by the National Institutes of Health and the Carnegie Corporation of New York, Pelz and associates at the University of Michigan began a six-year study with the question, "What constitutes a stimulating atmosphere for research and development?" (Pelz and Andrews 1966, p. 1). Including Ph.D.'s in research laboratories in universities in their sample, they addressed their research to those factors associated with high research performance, such as motivation, communication, age, and freedom. As a result, their findings became important baseline information for numerous analyses of correlates of research productivity in the years to follow.

At approximately the same time, another line of research emerged that provided a theoretical base for future performance studies. Robert Merton at Columbia University began work on the social structure of institutions and the general orientations characterizing its participants (Storer 1973). Merton studied the norms associated with scientific work in science, patterns of competition among scientists, the reward structure of science, scholarly refereeing, and inequality in scientific performance (Merton and Gaston 1977). These studies added substance and depth to a field of study known today as the sociology of science. They also spawned numerous studies of scientific research performance by Merton's students and colleagues: Zuckerman's (1977) study of Nobel laureates; Jonathan and Stephen Cole's (1973) examination of social stratification in sciences; Crane's (1965) analysis of productivity and scholarly recognition; Crane's advisee at Yale, Gaston's (1978) study of reward systems; Hagstrom's (1965) work at Berkeley on scientific communities. From the early 1960s to the present, these authors and their studies have provided a theoretical base for the study of research performance from the sociology-of-science literature.

Purpose and Scope of Study

This study reviews the literature on faculty research performance using four questions as an organizing framework: How is research performance, especially high research performance, measured? What explanations exist for why some faculty become prolific research producers? What specific correlates (or factors) influence high research performance? And what are the implications for faculty development, faculty evaluation, and future research?

No common agreement exists among writers as to the proper term to use to describe varying levels of faculty research. Sociologists and management specialists use the terms "scientific performance" (e.g., Andrews 1979), "scientific productivity" (e.g., Folger, Astin, and Bayer 1970), or "research performance" or "output" (e.g., Jauch and Glueck 1975). For consistency and simplicity, this discussion uses the terms "research productivity" and "research performance" interchangeably.

Admittedly, these two terms are open to several interpretations. "Performance" or "productivity" can imply a high level or abundance (i.e., a large quantity) of output (Hicks 1978–79). But, of course, the precise level varies by discipline, field, and institution. According to Blume and Sinclair (1973), whether an individual is productive should be assessed by peers competent to judge. "Research" is equally vague. The term can be subsumed under the general concept "scholarly work," which Braxton and Toombs (1982) discussed as the application or use of knowledge and skills acquired through and certified by doctoral research training. Specific "research" activities may be broadly conceived as the 22 activities cited by the National Center for Higher Education Management Systems (Manning and Romney 1973). Or it can be narrowly conceived to include submitting an article for publication in an academic or professional journal; publishing an article in an academic or professional journal; publishing or editing, alone or in collaboration, a book or monograph; publishing a book review; or delivering a paper at a professional meeting (Pellino, Blackburn, and Boberg 1984). For purposes of this discussion, "research" assumes varied forms, and "productivity" and "performance" are defined as high or exemplary output, such output being determined within academic departments, colleges, and institutions.

This review examines only *individual* faculty research performance. Analyses of departmental, collegial, or institutional research performance are available elsewhere (e.g., Kroc 1983; Wallhaus 1975). Also, this study is limited to "research" productivity, acknowledging that faculty performance encompasses service and teaching as well as research (e.g., Kirschling 1979; Yuker 1978). Only studies in the sciences and social sciences are reviewed: few discussions are available in the literature for other disciplines, such as the arts and humanities. Finally, this study draws heavily on the literature on the sociology of science and data-based results from sociological studies.

A discussion of the problems relating to the measurement of faculty productivity must start out with the recognition of the fact that there are many problems involved in this type of measurement (Yuker 1978, p. 46).

Although writers in the literature do not agree on which measures of individual research performance are most appropriate, they use three common measures: publication counts, citation counts, and peer and colleague ratings (Folger, Astin, and Bayer 1970). *Publication counts,* which measure the *quantity* of individual output, may include papers presented at professional meetings, journal articles, monographs, chapters in books, and books written alone or in collaboration. *Citations,* which measure the *quality* of a publication and its "influence" on academic knowledge, are reflected in the number of times others cite it, as reported in published citation indices, such as the *Science Citation Index* (Cole, J. and Zuckerman 1984; Folger, Astin, and Bayer 1970). *Ratings,* by peers or colleagues, measure the *reputation* of a scholar or researcher in the academic community (Cole, J. 1979). Ratings often include an assessment of the perceived quality and visibility of research and the perceived contribution to general knowledge in the field (Cole, J. 1979; Pelz and Andrews 1966). Researchers gather ratings from questionnaires, letters, or interviews (Cole, J. 1979; Pelz and Andrews 1966).

The three measures are intercorrelated. Faculty prolific in publishing produce works that are heavily cited. This fact has been supported by studies establishing positive correlations in the range of $r = .50$ to $r = .75$ between citation and publication counts, depending on the sample (Cole, J. and Zuckerman 1984). Being cited is not only a by-product of copious publications: It also stems from major papers receiving much attention. Jonathan Cole and Zuckerman (1984) found that the more prolific the scientists were in publishing, the more citations their *most cited* paper received.

Citations are also positively correlated with peer ratings. Faculty peers use the works of those faculty who achieve prominence or are prominent in their field (Cole, J. 1979). Cole found that visibility with peers correlates positively

. . . The more prolific the scientists were in publishing, the more citations their most cited paper received.

with publishing-productivity rates (ranging from $r = .37$ to $r = .56$) and with citation counts (ranging from $r = .45$ to $r = .63$).

Research performance can be measured in ways other than publication counts, citation counts, and ratings. These include research grants obtained, appointments to editorial boards (i.e., eminence measures), and the development of patents, improved processes, new products, or new analytic methods (see Centra 1977; Jauch and Glueck 1975; McPherson 1963; and Seldin 1984a). However, these measures are little used in productivity studies. A random sample of productivity studies showed that the criterion measures used are publication counts, citation counts, a combination of publication and citation counts, and to a lesser extent, ratings (see Table 1).

Publication Counts
A popular measure for determining research performance is publication counts (Folger, Astin, and Bayer 1970). Caplow and McGee (1958) suggest that evaluation of performance is based almost exclusively on publications in scholarly books or journals. When they asked 371 interviewees the question, "Do you think he has reached the peak of his productivity as yet?", 122 of the respondents defined productivity as research or publication of research, 14 referred either directly or indirectly to teaching, and the other 235 were not specific about their definition. Caplow and McGee concluded, then, that "the explicit definition of publication as the criterion of productivity is very common" (p. 70).

Two common ways to measure publication or bibliographic counts are "straight counts" (Lindsey 1980) and weighted counts. "Straight counts" report the number of published journal articles, books, and monographs. Researchers can identify the number of journal articles written by a particular person through an author search of the ERIC system (Kroc 1983). They can also ask faculty to report their publications on a questionnaire. Wanner, Lewis, and Gregorio (1981) used this latter approach based on the 1972–73 national survey conducted by the American Council on Education (ACE). Though the authors admitted that self-reported measures are crude and that the researchers built no safeguards into the ACE survey to

TABLE 1
RESEARCH PERFORMANCE MEASURES

Study	Data Collection

Publication Counts

Study	Data Collection
Crane (1965)	index based on interview data
Clemente (1973)	Glenn & Villemez (1970) Comprehensive Index (GVCI)
Astin (1978)	self-reported publications in ACE's 1972–73 national survey
Blackburn, Behymer, & Hall (1978)	self-reported publications in ACE/Carnegie Commission's 1969 national survey (Bayer 1970)
Cole, S. (1979)	counts in *Science Citation Index*
Knorr et al. (1979)	self-reported number of papers published
Cameron & Blackburn (1981)	weighted scale for publications drawn from vitae
Wanner, Lewis, & Gregorio (1981)	self-reported articles and books in ACE's 1972–73 national survey
Creswell, Barnes, & Wendel (1982)	self-reported publications in Ladd & Lipset's (1978) national survey, 1977

Citation Counts

Study	Data Collection
Folger, Astin, & Bayer (1970)	*Science Citation Index*

Publication and Citation Counts

Study	Data Collection
Cole, J. & Cole, S. (1973)	number of papers in *Science Abstract;* citations in *Science Citation Index*
Allison & Stewart (1974)	self-reported information; *Chemical Abstracts; Science Citation Index*
Hargens (1978)	*Science Citation Index* and review of journals
Long (1978)	publications in *Chemical Abstracts;* Citations in *Science Citation Index*
Reskin (1978)	self-reported publication counts; *Science Citation Index* counts

Ratings

Study	Data Collection
Pelz & Andrews (1966)	ratings by senior researchers in laboratory
Cole, J. (1979)	peer assessments made through questionnaires

check for the accuracy of self-reported information, they hastened to add that questionnaire research is commonplace in sociological studies.

Gathering self-reported data may cost less than other research techniques. Also, researchers can estimate the reliability of self-reported information. For example, Allison and Stewart (1974) estimated the reliability of responses from chemists in their sample by comparing self-reported information with publication counts from *Chemical Abstracts*. The correlation was r = .94, which suggests that the data were reliable.

Clemente (1972) reviewed studies incorporating weighted publication counts. In this procedure articles and books are given an arbitrary number of points. For example, Lightfield (1971) assigned 1 point for an article, 1 point for an edited book, and 1 point per 100 pages of an original book; Manis (1951) awarded 1 point for articles and edited books, 18 points for single-author books, and partial credit for coauthored books. After reviewing 10 studies that used different weighting schemes, Clemente (1972) suggested the adoption of a standard index for measuring sociological productivity. He recommended the Glenn and Villemez (1970) weighting scheme because it contained a quality rating of journals derived through consensus by sociologists. The Glenn and Villemez index assigned 30 points to research and theoretical monographs, 15 points to textbooks (including revisions), 10 points to edited books, and from 4 to 10 points for articles in journals, depending on the quality of the journal (e.g., 10 points for articles in the *American Sociological Review* and the *American Journal of Sociology*). The Glenn and Villemez index implies that a weighting scheme should be based on values assigned only within specific academic fields or disciplines. A reasonable and acceptable weighting scheme across fields could be unreliable because faculty in disparate disciplines emphasize different forms of publication (e.g., journal articles in chemistry and books in political science) (Biglan 1973).

The accuracy of both weighted counts and straight counts is limited in other ways. When researchers count publications they may give equal credit to poorly conceived papers appearing in badly edited journals and to well-written papers in high-quality journals (Smith and Fiedler 1971). In addition, they may compare counts from disciplines with many publication outlets with those from disciplines with few outlets. They may count the contributions of coauthors the same as contributions of single authors and consider the value of a shorter paper to be the same as that of a longer paper. And they may give more weight to the "operator" who produces quantity than the scholar who produces quality (Bayer and Folger 1966; Smith and Fiedler 1971).

Citation Counts

An emphasis on the quality of a publication has stimulated the use of citation counts as a measure of research performance. This approach assumes that a cited study has significantly influenced the body of scientific knowledge (Folger, Astin, and Bayer 1970). Citation counts correlate highly with other measures of quality, such as employment in a prestigious university, listing in important bibliographies of scientists, and receiving scientific awards and recognition by colleagues, for example, the National Medal of Science, the Thorndike Award in psychology, and a Nobel prize (Kroc 1983; Lindsey 1980).

Citation counts are a "natural weighting" of written and accessible scholarly works, and they may be the single best measure of scientific achievement (Folger, Astin, and Bayer 1970, p. 257). Researchers base citation counts on information provided by citation indices developed in the past 20 years. Three popular indices are the *Science Citation Index* (SCI), the *Social Science Citation Index* (SSCI), and the *Arts and Humanities Citation Index* (Garfield 1979). The *Journal Citation Report,* published every third year, supplements the SCI and SSCI by providing data on journals covered by the indices (Kroc 1984).

All scientific papers include citations for elaboration, establishment of precedent, or for illustration. From the indices (e.g., SCI), which contain an author reference, a researcher can determine how many times an author's works are cited. If an author's work is valuable, others will refer to it. For example, in an early pilot study of the use of citation measures, Bayer and Folger (1966) analyzed the research performance of 467 biochemists using citation counts in the 1964 *Science Citation Index,* which reported on 27 source journals in biochemistry. From the SCI they identified the number of times each biochemist's publications were cited. Abstracts, book reviews, theses, corrections, editorials, and such items as letters and personal correspondence, as well as self-citations, were excluded from the counts. The result was a count of the number of citations the authors of the studies in the 1964 journals made to the published scholarly works of the biochemists.

Collecting citation counts is easy because of the availability of citation indices. Citations also minimize the effects of an author's personality or employing institution on performance, are less subject to personal manipulation than other measures of research performance, and remain stable over time (Bayer and Folger 1966; Kroc 1983; Lindsey 1980; Smith and Fiedler 1971).

Most authors acknowledge the shortcomings of citation analysis (Kroc 1984; Lindsey 1978). Citations are susceptible to fads and popular trends because researchers cite certain works frequently. Citations may also be biased toward statistical and methodological studies routinely cited regardless of impact on the substance of an article. Lindsey (1980) pointed out that when social scientists use a popular statistic, they feel compelled to cite the elementary statistical text from which they learned it. Citation indices cite works by first author, which makes it difficult for researchers to determine collaborative authorship. In addition, citations may not reflect current works of quality because of the lag between publication and citation. Jonathan Cole and Zuckerman (1984, p. 240) raise additional concerns about the accuracy of citation counts:

> *Does a work cited an average of 55 times over 12 years have a greater impact than a work cited an average of 32 times over 12 years? Or, have two scientists who have each been cited 50 times in a given year had the same impact when one has published 25 papers, each of which has been cited twice, and the other has also published 25 papers but has two papers which received 25 citations each, while the other 23 received none at all?*

Not only is there confusion in interpreting the impact of a single paper or set of papers, but also in determining whether citations provide incentives to continue publishing and whether citations are an accurate measure of the "influence" of a work. Just how much publication is necessary before a scientific contribution becomes visible? And at what point do scientists' publications "clutter" the literature?

Ratings of Performance

A final measure of research performance is rating by peers within and outside the institution; by departmental chairs, deans, personnel committees; or by one's self (Centra 1977; Seldin 1984a). Ratings reflect an individual's "reputation," and a researcher's reputation affects his or her impact in shaping the cognitive content of a field, whether this impact is as a gatekeeper of ideas or as a developer of a research area or specialty (Cole, J. 1979). It also determines rewards, such as employment opportunities from other universities or large research grants from funding agencies.

Jonathan Cole's study (1979) illustrated the use of peer ratings as a criterion measure of research performance. He examined the research reputations of faculty in sociology, psychology, and four biological-science specialities in American universities that grant doctorates. The study employed two dependent measures of reputational standing as evaluated by peers working in the same discipline: the perceived quality and the visibility of scientific research. Cole asked respondents to evaluate the importance of the work produced by a stratified random sample of scientists in their own field by using a six-point scale ranging from "has made very important contributions" to "have never heard of this scientist." He measured individual visibility by the percentage of all respondents who thought they had enough information to rate the person.

Measurement of research performance by ratings has many advantages. Ratings are a traditional method for evaluating faculty research performance in deciding promotion and tenure. Ratings can reflect an individual's market worth, when peers off-campus esteem an individual's research. Ratings are also highly related to other measures of performance, such as citation counts and positions held in professional associations (Clark 1957). And ratings may be a good measure of performance because peers know the researcher's work and consider themselves qualified to compare it with the work of others (Pelz and Andrews 1966).

On the other hand, because ratings are based on perceptions, they may be flawed by inadequate or false information. They may reflect the quality of the institution in which the researcher is employed (the "halo effect"). Moreover, ratings are inherently "intersubjective," that is, peers and colleagues will apply different subjective criteria to reach the conclusion that an individual "has made very important contributions" (Cole, J. 1979; Folger, Astin, and Bayer 1970; Pelz and Andrews 1966). These weaknesses influence the popularity of ratings as a way of measuring research performance, and few studies in the literature actually employ the measure as a criterion.

Summary
Of the various measures of research performance in the literature, the most common have been publication counts, citation counts, and ratings by peers and colleagues. Researchers count the number of publications of a scholar (e.g., journal articles, books, monographs) through "straight counts," obtained from self-reported information or by reviewing an educational data base such as ERIC, or through a weighting procedure that assigns arbitrary weights to types of publications. Researchers gather citation counts using citation indices developed in the past 20 years, such as the *Science Citation Index* or the *Social Science Citation Index*. Using these indices, researchers can obtain information about the total number of times individuals or their works are cited by others. Research performance can also be measured by peer or colleague ratings. Peers or colleagues can evaluate the reputation of an individual's research by responding to a questionnaire, interview, or letter.

Researchers do not agree on a common measure of research performance. Rather, research performance seems to be a multidimensional concept (Yuker 1978), frequently measured by publication and citation counts, and to a lesser extent, by peer or colleague ratings.

CONCEPTUAL EXPLANATIONS OF RESEARCH PERFORMANCE

The number of publications scientists produce varies enormously, whether one looks at a year's production, or a five-year period, or a lifetime. And most of this variation has never been explained in any published paper on the subject. That situation makes scientific productivity one of the most difficult and perplexing problems in the sociology of science (Gaston 1978, p. 133).

The average rate of faculty publication tends to be low and the variation in performance levels very high (Fox 1983). In 1926, Lotka advanced a mathematical distribution of performance rates in his inverse-square rule of scientific productivity. According to Lotka's rule, the number of people producing n scientific papers is proportional to $1/n^2$, that is, for every 100 authors who produce a single paper in a specific period, there are 25 who produce two, 11 with three, and so on (Price 1963). This means that 6 percent of the scientific community produces 50 percent of the scientific publications, or the average scientist publishes only about three papers in a lifetime (MacRoberts and Mac-Roberts 1982; Price 1963).

Recent statistics from national surveys of the professoriate confirm that many faculty publish few papers. As shown in Table 2, 31 percent of the respondents (N = 5,000) to Ladd and Lipset's (1978) *Survey of the American Professoriate* published from zero to four journal articles during their careers; in 1969, 59 percent of the respondents to the American Council on Education-Carnegie Commission survey (N = 60,000) reported publishing from zero to four journal articles. In contrast, prolific publishers, such as Nobel laureates, according to Zuckerman's 1977 study, publish an average of 13.1 papers before they reach the young age of 30. A matched sample of less distinguished scientists from *American Men of Science* produced an average of only 3.1 papers. Theodore Cockerell, a noted entomologist, published a stunning record of 3,904 papers during his career. He produced about two papers a week at his peak (Zuckerman 1970).

Why do some faculty succeed in publishing widely acclaimed works year after year, while other scientists publish almost nothing (Long 1978)? Four explanations are commonly discussed in the literature: psychological-

Recent statistics from national surveys of the professoriate confirm that many faculty publish few papers.

TABLE 2
JOURNAL ARTICLES PUBLISHED IN UNIVERSITIES AS REPORTED BY NATIONAL SURVEYS

Total Journal Articles Published	American Council on Education & Carnegie Comm., 1969 (Bayer 1970)	American Council on Education, 1972–73 (Bayer 1973)	Ladd & Lipset, 1977 (Ladd & Lipset 1978)
None	29.5%	24.0%	9.4%
1–4	29.7	25.9	21.9
5–10	14.1	16.1	19.9
11–20	10.3	14.0	18.6
21 +	16.3	19.9	30.3

individual, cumulative advantage, reinforcement, and disciplinary norms. Unfortunately, no single study reviews all four explanations, though Fox (1983) perceptively analyzed individual, environmental, and feedback (i.e., cumulative advantage and reinforcement) explanations. And Gaston (1978) and Allison and Stewart (1974) discussed the cumulative advantage, psychological, and reinforcement explanations.

Psychological-Individual Explanations
The psychological-individual explanation suggests that productive researchers possess certain psychological and individual characteristics that are absent in less productive researchers. Sociologists who have ventured into the domain of psychology have explored this idea (see Fox 1983), as well as psychologists who have studied "creativity" (see Taylor and Barron 1963).

A first variant of the psychological-individual explanation is that productive researchers may possess "innate" scientific ability or talent. Success or failure, then, is largely determined by the quality of native intelligence (Cole, J., and Cole, S. 1973), measurable by standard I.Q. tests (Cox 1980). I.Q. tests, however, as well as other standardized measures of intelligence may be only a rough indicator of ability, and it is doubtful whether intelligence is as unequally distributed among the population of faculty in higher education as is research performance (Fox 1983). Besides, evidence suggests that an insignificant negative correlation exists between I.Q. and scientific achievement (Bayer and Folger 1966).

A second variant is the "sacred spark" explanation, which maintains that faculty engage in research because they have a strong inner compulsion or motivation. According to Jonathan and Stephen Cole (1973, p. 62):

> *Some scientists, no doubt, would continue to work hard on their research even if the norms prescribed that the researcher must remain anonymous. These scientists have the "sacred spark." They are motivated by an inner drive to do science and by a sheer love of the work.*

Eminent scientists are highly motivated, intellectually self-reliant, and confident in their ideas (Merton 1973; Pelz and Andrews 1966). A "spark" may be a function of the socialization process of science, because the process tends to produce people who are strongly committed to science. For them,

> *research as an activity comes to be "natural" . . . they find it self-evident that persons should be excited by discoveries, intensely interested in the detailed working of nature, and committed to the elaboration of theories that are of no use whatever in daily life* (Hagstrom 1965, p. 9).

A third variant includes explanations based on the personality traits of researchers. Biographical studies of eminent scientists reveal hardworking people who possess certain cognitive structures (i.e., play with ideas, recombine familiar concepts, and tolerate ambiguity and abstraction) and have identifiable emotional characteristics (e.g., high ego strength, personal dominance) (Fox 1983; Roe 1953). Since certain stresses may relate to personality, researchers are exploring the relationship between faculty stress levels (e.g., life events, family problems, attitudes toward job) and number of scholarly publications (Horowitz, Blackburn, and Edington 1984).

A fourth variant explains research performance by background or personal characteristics. Sociologists have explored gender differences and productivity (e.g., see Cole, J. 1979). There is conclusive evidence that men publish more than women, but the literature is not as clear about the reasons for the differential output (and citations)

(Cole, J. and Zuckerman 1984). One possibility is that women may publish less than men because they are isolated from the "old boy" network and not in touch with the "invisible college" through which scientific information is exchanged. Moreover, women's work is not taken seriously by the academic community; their work often focuses on topics deemed insignificant by those in positions of power (though Jonathan Cole and Zuckerman 1984 contend that men may "clutter" the literature more than women) (Astin 1984). Women scientists seem more readily discouraged and less readily encouraged by varying degrees of citation to their work (Cole, J. and Zuckerman 1984). And traditional family obligations of women prevent them from spending as much time working on research as men, though Stephen Cole (1979) has found that the stability and routinism associated with marriage are actually positively correlated with high publication rates.

Another background characteristic used to explain high research performance is age. The literature on age and productivity is largely atheoretical (Reskin 1980). The relevant literature supports conflicting assumptions: growing old impairs performance, though performance improves with experience (and with age). One might argue that age impairs human performance because of psychological or mental decline or personality changes that interfere with performance. On the other hand, as faculty age, they gain valuable experience that should lead to improved performance. The negative and the positive impacts of aging could indeed cancel each other out or operate separately at different stages of a professional career (Reskin 1980). Reskin (1980) suggested several factors that affect the relationship between aging and research performance: motivation, risk-taking, stamina, socialization to research norms, the organizational reward system (including the monetary rewards for research), social position, competing demands on a scientist's time, extraprofessional roles (e.g., commitment to family), and the effect of scientific specialties.

Cumulative Advantage
Another explanation for research productivity, drawn from sociology more than psychology, is "cumulative advantage." When the performance of faculty measures up to or exceeds institutional standards, a process of "cumulative

advantage" is initiated whereby "the individual acquires successively enlarged opportunities to advance his work (and the rewards that go with it) even further" (Merton and Gaston 1977, p. 89). The idea is based on Merton's (1973) "Matthew effect" in science: once scientists receive recognition (or resources) from their colleagues, they accrue additional advantages as they progress through their careers. This effect derived its name from a passage in the Gospel of Matthew, "For unto every one that hath shall be given, and he shall have abundance: but from him that hath not shall be taken away even that which he hath" (Merton 1973, p. 445).

The advantages typically begin with doctoral training in a prestigious department. The training, in turn, leads to a position in a major research university amply supplied with adequate resources for research (Long and McGinnis 1981). Jonathan and Stephen Cole (1973) described the overall impact of the advantages:

> By virtue of being in top graduate departments and interacting with influential and brilliant scientists, some scientists have a social advantage in the process of stratification. Once position has been established in this initial phase, the probabilities may no longer be the same for two scientists of equal abilities. The one who is strategically located in the stratification system may have a series of accumulating advantages over the one who is not a member of the elite corps (pp. 74–75).

Studies of graduate-training experiences, employment in prestigious institutions, and resources available for research have tested this explanation (e.g., Allison and Stewart 1974; Cole, J. and Cole, S. 1973; Merton 1973). It is a common explanation in the literature on the sociology of science and is found juxtaposed with the psychological "sacred spark" explanation in several studies (Allison and Stewart 1974; Cole, J. and Cole, S. 1973).

Reinforcement

Cumulative advantage is often confused with reinforcement as an explanation of productivity (Fox 1983). Both are derivatives of the "Matthew effect" and are related to recognition. But the two explanations are conceptually distinct: cumulative advantage deals with resources, prestigious doctoral departments, and so forth; reinforcement addresses the feedback one receives from successful publication of works, works being cited, and formal and informal praise from colleagues. The reinforcement explanation holds that when faculty publish, the recognition they receive for the contribution stimulates further publication (Gaston 1978). Thus, recognition motivates authors to publish because it affirms an individual's personal worth. Although recognition may assume many forms, a common form is citations to published works. The Skinnerian behaviorist principle is that an activity that is rewarded continues to be performed, while an activity not rewarded tends to be dropped. Jonathan and Stephen Cole (1973) described the application of the idea to physics:

> *Soon after they receive their degrees (and sometimes before), these young physicists begin to publish their research, whether alone or as part of a research team. . . . standards are high, and the manuscripts even of eminent scientists are sometimes rejected. Even though standards employed by the journals are high, a majority of papers are accepted for publication. More important than the formal evaluation of journals is the informal evaluation after publication by the international community of physicists. Sometimes the published paper is largely ignored, with few citations to it, or it may be identified as a significant contribution and put to use in many other published researches. If the reward system, in the form of recognition by citation, does affect research productivity, we assume that the greater such collegial recognition of these early researches by physicists, the greater the probability that the physicists will continue to be productive. We hypothesize that few scientists will continue to engage in research if they are not rewarded for it* (pp. 111–112).

Several writers using different measures of recognition have confirmed the importance of reinforcement. Using citations, Jonathan and Stephen Cole (1973) determined that the more citations to early works, the more likely physicists are to continue being productive. Using early publications (i.e., publications accepted soon after receipt of the doctorate), Meltzer (1949–50), Manis (1951), and Lightfield (1971) reported that early producers continue to maintain high levels of productivity throughout their careers. With great confidence Lightfield (1971) claimed, "Unless a person achieves a qualitative piece of research during his first five years as a sociologist . . . it seems unlikely that he will do so during his next five years—if at any time during his career" (p. 133). Using rate of publication as a surrogate measure of reinforcement, Blackburn, Behymer, and Hall (1978) found prior publications positively correlated with career publications, thus confirming a "habit of writing" that develops early in an individual's career and carries through to later life. This "habit" may be a result of a reinforcement process whereby the reward system encourages research activities (Cole, S. and Cole, J. 1967; Fox 1983; Lightfield 1971).

Of all the explanations for research performance, reinforcement may be the most important . . .

Another aspect of reinforcement is the informal recognition given to a scholar by colleagues. Gaston (1978) and Reskin (1977) attributed productivity to the *immediate reinforcement* that researchers received from colleagues rather than to the delayed reinforcement of having their works cited. Such reinforcement may include promotion in rank or the conferring of tenure. Reskin (1977) discussed collegial recognition:

> *In such contexts (research-oriented institutions), immediate informal recognition from research-oriented colleagues may be more important in maintaining productivity than the formal, but delayed recognition that citations provide. . . . Given the reward structure of most university departments, the act of publishing—signalling both successful professional performance and a variety of forthcoming rewards—may be especially reinforcing to university scientists* (p. 502).

Of all the explanations for research performance, reinforcement may be the most important because of the strong positive relationship between its measures (e.g., prior productivity) and high performance levels.

Disciplinary Norms
Colleagues and the disciplinary environment shape research performance. As one historian of science

TABLE 3
SELECTED STUDIES OF FACULTY RESEARCH PRODUCTIVITY, SINGLE AND MULTIPLE DISCIPLINES AND NATIONAL DATA BASES

Selected Studies	Single Discipline	Multiple Disciplines	National Data Base
Allison & Stewart (1974)		biologists, mathematicians, chemists, physicists	
Astin (1978)			ACE 1972–73 survey
Babchuk & Bates (1962)	sociologists		
Bayer & Folger (1966)	biochemists		
Blackburn, Behymer, & Hall (1978)			ACE/Carnegie Commission 1969 survey
Braxton (1983)		chemists, psychologists	
Cameron & Blackburn (1981)		English, psychologists, sociologists	
Clemente (1973)	sociologists		
Cole, J. & Cole, S. (1973)		physical, biological, and social scientists	
Cole, S. (1979)			ACE 1972–73 survey
Crane (1965)		biologists, political scientists, psychologists	
Creswell, Barnes, & Wendel (1982)			Ladd & Lipset 1977 survey
Creswell, Patterson, & Barnes (1984a, b)			Ladd & Lipset 1977 survey
Fulton & Trow (1974)			Carnegie Commission 1969 survey
Hargens (1978)		chemists, mathematicians, politicial scientists	
Hargens, McCann, & Reskin (1978)	chemists		

TABLE 3 (continued)

Selected Studies	Single Discipline	Multiple Disciplines	National Data Base
Knorr et al. (1979)			UNESCO Int'l comparative study
Lightfield (1971)	sociologists		
Long & McGinnis (1981)	biochemists		
Long (1978)	biochemists		
Manis (1951)		social scientists	
Meltzer (1949–50)		social scientists	
Pelz & Andrews (1966)		biological, physical, social scientists	
Reskin (1979)	chemists		
Wanner, Lewis, & Gregorio (1981)			ACE 1972–73 survey

remarked, "The study of science, after all, begins with its product, scientific knowledge, rather than simply with those individuals who occupy the social position of 'scientist' " (Storer 1973, p. xvii). Thus, the norms of a discipline (or field of study), as well as scientific knowledge in the discipline, partially explain variations in faculty research performance. During the past 40 years studies have sampled faculty from single disciplines and multiple disciplines, and most major disciplines have been sampled in national surveys. (See Table 3.) In national surveys, researchers can compare faculty across disciplines and isolate the effects of discipline membership on performance (e.g., Blackburn, Behymer, and Hall 1978; Wanner, Lewis, and Gregorio 1981).

The norms of a discipline affect faculty research performance in two ways: by the degree of codification of knowledge (or stage of paradigm development) (Zuckerman and Merton 1973) and by differences in the research activities, called the social activities of disciplines by Gaston (1978). The codification of knowledge is best understood by reviewing Thomas Kuhn's (1970) classic treatment of paradigm structure in *The Structure of Scientific Revolutions*.

He described how fields in science are not uniformly developed. Fields differ in their stage of paradigmatic development: in the understanding of the accepted theory; in the preferred methodologies; and in the understanding of the important areas to study. According to Lodahl and Gordon (1972), the paradigm "provides structure by suggesting which problems require investigation next, what methods are appropriate to their study, and even which findings are indeed 'proven' " (p. 58). Disciplines are in different paradigmatic stages. Social sciences (e.g., political science) are immature fields and are considered to be in a pre-paradigmatic stage. The physical sciences (e.g., physics) are mature fields and in a paradigmatic stage.

The paradigmatic stage of a discipline affects scholarly research (Lodahl and Gordon 1972). It affects acceptance rates in journals: in fields in which the acceptance rates are high (e.g., physics), the degree of codification is high because individuals in the field agree on the important questions and approriate methods to address them (Gaston 1978; see also Whitely's 1977 discussion of "restricted" and "unrestricted" sciences). It also affects the form of communication: an abbreviated form of scholarly communication, journal articles, is permitted in disciplines in a paradigmatic stage, such as the physical sciences, and a lengthened form, books and monographs, is required in pre-paradigmatic fields, such as education (Biglan 1973).

Disciplines also differ in their research activities. Gaston (1978) outlined some of these differences: the amount of concern scientists express about being anticipated in their current research (the priority struggle); the age of the literature referred to by scientific papers; the average number of papers produced annually; the validity of published answers to research questions; the extent to which mathematics is used in research; the coauthorship patterns; the reliance on research assistants to make all or most of the observations and measurements; and the division of labor on manuscripts for which various collaborators supply special skills.

Certainly, other factors are also important. Though researchers know about differences in the cognitive structure and research activities of disciplines, they have yet to explore the exact impact of those differences on productivity. Few studies directly address this impact (an exception being Biglan 1973), and most include academic discipline as a control variable (e.g., Wanner, Lewis, and Gregorio 1981) in the assessment of correlates associated with productivity.

Summary
The research performance of faculty in higher education is highly variable. Most of the scholarly research is being produced by a few faculty. Thus, productivity researchers attempt to explain the variation in faculty research performance by psychological-individual factors, including superior intellectual ability (innate ability); a strong motivation and drive to perform (sacred spark); personality traits; and background characteristics, such as gender and age. Another explanation is the "cumulative advantage" argument, which is based on the idea that some faculty accrue resources and the advantages of position whereas other faculty do not. These resources and advantages, in turn, contribute to high levels of productivity. Finally, high performance levels result from the positive reinforcement some faculty receive for their works and from the norms and expectations of their disciplines.

CORRELATES OF RESEARCH PERFORMANCE

Effective research is a product, first, of a sociocultural climate; second, of a sufficiency of individuals gifted with an uncommon combination of abilities and character qualities; third, of a satisfactory economic-administrative matrix; fourth, of special acquired research skills and thought processes; and last, of daily working conditions which, at the least, must not hamper creative minds (Cattell, 1963, p. 199).

Writers have examined the explanations of faculty research performance using a complex set of correlates (or factors). Numerous studies report correlates of research performance in sociology, psychology, and, to a lesser extent, education in the past 40 years. These studies examine a common core of correlates, and they can be related generally to the explanations discussed earlier, as shown in Table 4 (see p. 28). The relationship is not perfect, however, because some correlates can be used to test several explanations (e.g., academic rank leads to cumulative advantage as well as recognition and reinforcement from peers). Most of the correlate studies are multivariate in design, and the authors examine the relative influence of each correlate independently (e.g., see Blackburn, Behymer, and Hall 1978; Clemente 1973; Fox 1983; Wanner, Lewis, and Gregorio 1981). A few of the correlate studies use a bivariate design to examine the relationship between one correlate and research performance (e.g., Holley 1977). Complex causal models are reported in Reskin's (1979) test of the effect of academic sponsorship on scientists' decade productivity (i.e., 10 years after doctorate), Knorr et al.'s (1979) examination of a social-position model, and Bean's (1982) macro-organizational model. A wide array of correlates are reviewed by Clemente (1973) and Finkelstein (1984). In an excellent synthesis, Fox (1983) organizes the correlates in terms of individual-level characteristics (psychological characteristics, work habits, demographic characteristics), environmental location, and feedback processes. Some writers also indicate methodological problems associated with the use of correlates (Bayer and Dutton 1977; Reskin 1980).

This discussion reviews the major correlates reported in research-productivity studies, Specific measures are identi-

TABLE 4
CORRELATES OF FACULTY RESEARCH PRODUCTIVITY

Variables	Selected Studies
Psychological-Individual Explanation	
Intelligence scores	Bayer & Folger (1966); Folger, Astin, & Bayer (1970)
Motivation	Gaston (1978); Hunter & Kuh (1984); Pelz & Andrews (1966)
Personality characteristics	Fox (1983); Roe (1953); Taylor & Ellison (1967)
Stress	Gmelch, Wilke, & Lovrich (1984); Horowitz, Blackburn, & Edington (1984); McKeachie (1983)
Age	Bayer & Dutton (1977); Blackburn & Havighurst (1979); Cole, S. (1979); Creswell, Patterson, & Barnes (1984a); Lehman (1953); Over (1982); Pelz & Andrews (1966)
Gender	Astin (1978); Babchuk & Bates (1966); Blackburn, Behymer, & Hall (1978); Cameron & Blackburn (1981); Folger, Astin, & Bayer (1970); Hargens, McCann, & Reskin (1978)
Cumulative Advantage Explanation	
Prestige of doctoral program	Crane (1965); Reskin (1979)
Mentoring	Cameron & Blackburn (1981); Long (1978); Reskin (1979)
Prestige of employing institution	Crane (1965); Long & McGinnis (1981)
Resources and assignment	Allison & Stewart (1974); Knorr et al. (1979); Pelz & Andrews (1966)
Reinforcement Explanation	
Colleagues	Braxton (1983); Collins (1971); Finkelstein (1982); Parker, Lingwood, & Paisley (1968); Pelz & Andrews (1966)
Academic rank and tenure	Blackburn, Behymer, & Hall (1978); Creswell, Patterson, & Barnes (1984a); Holley (1977); Neumann (1979)
Early productivity	Blackburn, Behymer, & Hall (1978); Clemente (1973); Cole, S. & Cole, J. (1973); Lightfield (1971); Manis (1951); Meltzer (1949–50); Reskin (1979)
Preference for research	Blackburn, Behymer, & Hall (1978); Creswell, Barnes, & Wendel (1982)
Disciplinary Norms Explanation	
Disciplinary differences	Biglan (1973); Creswell, Barnes, & Wendel (1982); Wanner, Lewis, & Gregorio (1981)

fied, potential problems arising from their use are discussed, and their overall power to predict high research performance is assessed.

Intelligence Test Scores
Intelligence, as measured by intelligence test scores, has little predictive influence on high research performance. Studies of doctoral-level biochemists in 1957 (Bayer and Folger 1966) and in 1964 (Folger, Astin, and Bayer 1970) reported low correlations between intelligence test scores and productivity, as measured by citation counts (correlations ranged from -.049 to + 1.0). In another study, Jonathan and Stephen Cole (1973) confirmed the low correlations between test scores and publication counts (r = .05) for physical, biological, and social scientists.

Low correlations may be attributable to inexact measures of ability (Cole, J. and Cole, S. 1973) or to a possible interaction between intelligence and environmental influences. Regarding the interaction effects, Jonathan and Stephen Cole (1973) established that I.Q. was significantly related to the prestige of a scientist's academic department. Whereas intelligent faculty are probably employed in prestigious departments, the impact of intelligence on productivity is attenuated by departmental influences. Job setting, over time, assumes greater and greater predictive power in regard to performance.

Motivation
The precise impact of individual motivation on research performance is unknown. Measures of motivation are imprecise (Gaston 1978). Since motives constantly change, measuring motivation after the fact is methodologically difficult. Intensity of motivation among scholars also varies, and it is difficult to separate individual motives from environmental influences (Gaston 1978). Despite these problems, however, faculty are more intrinsically motivated than extrinsically motivated to produce research. Pelz and Andrews (1966) found effective university research scientists to be motivated to produce by strong inner sources, the desire for freedom to follow one's ideas, and the stimulation from one's previous work. Those scientists who were consistently low producers relied on supervisors or advisors for their motivation. In another study, Hunter and

. . . Faculty are more intrinsically motivated than extrinsically motivated to produce research.

Kuh (1984) described "prolific" scholars in higher education and student personnel administration as individuals who placed little importance on extrinsic sources of motivation, such as salary incentives, and great importance on the genuine enjoyment of engaging in scholarly activities.

Personality Characteristics

Scholars may bring to their careers certain personality characteristics that predispose them to be high producers. Biographical sketches of distinguished scholars have identified these characteristics (Fox 1983). A well-known study is that of the Yale psychologist, Anne Roe (1953, 1972), who examined the life histories of 64 eminent male physical and social scientists. Her life histories revealed that these eminent scientists had certain characteristics in common: they were from families with fathers who were professionals; they existed on their own resources early in life (e.g., some lost a parent); they held intense private interests in their youth; and they became involved in "gadgeteering" early in life. In terms of their general personality structure, the eminent scientists relied on rational controls, were uncritical people, and spent their time thinking about things in a question-answer way.

In another study, Collins (1971) found that creative scientists could be distinguished from less creative scientists by their personality profiles: creative scientists were more exact, precise, reliable, intelligent, and introverted. Taylor and Ellison (1967) analyzed the personality characteristics of 2,000 scientists in the Office of the National Aeronautics and Space Administration. Biographical information showed productive scientists to be independent, not swayed by general consensus, intellectually oriented, and confident in their abilities. This last trait, confidence, is a distinguishing characteristic of "prolific" scholars in the field of higher education and student personnel administration, as well. Hunter and Kuh (1984) found that "prolific" scholars display a "confidence personality factor," including an easygoing temperament, sense of humor, and confidence.

Personality traits undoubtedly influence research performance, but they do not act in a vacuum. Social factors affect the translation of personality (or creativity) into innovative performance (Fox 1983). Thus, strong interactive effects exist among personality traits, social and organizational variables, and high research performance. Further research studies are needed to increase our understanding of the interactive effects.

Stress

The relationship of individual stress to research productivity is a recent area of investigation. McKeachie (1983) reviewed stressful events on the job that can result in lowered productivity: departmental chairs or administrators who are critical and unappreciative of good work, incompatible colleagues, and lack of respect by others for what one is doing. When these factors affect an individual's job, "displacement activities" set in, such as hobbies, involvement in community services, and consulting or moneymaking ventures. These activities are certainly not physically threatening. However, physiological reactions, such as high triglycerides, high cholesterol, and others, may result from stress and affect overall research performance (Horowitz, Blackburn, and Edington 1984). Also, failure to receive anticipated rewards and recognition in the workplace is a source of stress that may influence research productivity (Gmelch, Wilke, and Lovrich 1984).

Age

The precise relationship between age and research productivity is difficult to determine because of complex measurement and other methodological problems. Various studies use different measures of age: chronological age (Cole, S. 1979; Pelz and Andrews 1966); years of professional experience (Creswell, Patterson, and Barnes 1984a); number of years since receipt of the doctorate (Allison and Stewart 1974; Bayer and Dutton 1977); and a combination of academic rank and years of experience in higher education (Baldwin and Blackburn 1981). The use of different measures makes generalizations of results from one study to another difficult. The studies also report cross-sectional rather than longitudinal data, thereby possibly entangling the effects of age with the effects of cohorts (Cole, S. 1979; Reskin 1980). Cohorts may differ in research performance not simply because of age differences but also because the pressures to publish vary from one historical period to another. Acknowledging this entangling effect, authors

have turned to other data collection procedures, such as longitudinal designs (in which a cohort group is followed over several decades) or a combination of cross-sectional and longitudinal designs, called a cross-sequential approach (Over 1982). But even these designs are subject to sample attrition problems.

A further difficulty is identifying the true "age curve" between age and research productivity. One model holds that the "age curve" is curvilinear. Lehman (1953) found that scholarly achievement peaks in the late thirties and early forties and declines thereafter (Oliver Wendell Holmes, Jr., is said to have remarked, "If you haven't cut your name on the door of fame by the time you've reached 40, you might just as well put up your jackknife" (quoted on p. 186). The decline in performance after one's early forties was also established by Stephen Cole (1979) and Over (1982). The decline in productivity in mid-career was attributed to reduced motivation to do research and devoting less time to research.

Another model suggests that the relationship is bimodal or "saddle-shaped" (Pelz and Andrews 1966). Pelz and Andrews found that publication productivity peaks during the ages of 35 to 44 and 50 to 54. Bayer and Dutton (1977) also confirmed this relationship; a "spurt-obsolescence curve" best fitted five of seven disciplines they studied. They attibuted the two-peak curve to changing market conditions and to the attrition of productive scientists away from academia during the second half of their careers and their return to faculty positions late in life. Pelz and Andrews (1966) ascribed the decline in middle years to a lack of "zeal or motivation" and a "fresh viewpoint" (p. 197).

A third possibility for the "true" age curve is discussed by Hammel (1980) and Creswell, Patterson, and Barnes (1984b). This curve is one of a gradually decelerating increase, thus confirming that productivity increases with age and that there is some evidence of a flattening, but not necessarily a decline. This curve may better fit high producers than low producers (Creswell, Patterson, and Barnes 1984b).

The best "age curve" is probably a function of the sample being studied (see Bayer and Dutton 1977) and the criterion measures of age and productivity used (Reskin

1980). These qualifications aside, various monotonic functions (e.g., "obsolescence," "spurt," and "spurt-obsolescence") or a bimodal curve, represented by a peak in performance about 10 years after the doctorate and a second peak toward the end of a faculty career, best describe the relationship between age and research (Reskin 1980).

Age, by itself, has little predictive influence on performance: variables highly related to age more precisely explain productivity than does age itself. Bayer and Dutton (1977) could explain only 7 percent of the variance in research productivity with age; Over (1982) found age to be an insignificant correlate when productivity was regressed against sex, academic rank, prior publication rate, and research standing of the university. Blackburn, Behymer, and Hall (1978) eliminated age entirely in their final statistical analysis because age correlated highly with academic rank.

Age, however, exercises an important mediating influence as a correlate of research performance. Blackburn and Havighurst (1979) examined the productivity of 74 U.S. male scientists born between 1893 and 1903. They divided scientists age 55 and older into four groups of producers and examined the correlates of productivity for each group. They concluded that an early start in publishing and the work environment of the scholar significantly influenced the 74 research careers. In another study, Creswell, Patterson, and Barnes (1984a) divided a national sample of faculty into four career-age groups similar to those used by Bayer and Dutton (1977). They then examined the significant correlates at each career age and found that some factors remained stable during the careers of faculty (e.g., time and preference for research, membership in select disciplines) but that others fluctuated (e.g., feelings about success, importance of rank attained).

Gender
Three questions are apparent in studies relating gender to research productivity: (1) whether one gender publishes more than the other; (2) whether the correlates of research productivity differ dramatically for women and men; and (3) whether gender *per se* is an important correlate of high research performance.

Men are generally more published and cited than women. In a study of 262 sociologists, Babchuk and Bates (1962) reported that women were far less prolific in publication than men and were overrepresented in the low-publication categories. Only 2 of the 37 women in the sample had published more than five articles. Astin (1969), in a study of faculty who responded to the American Council on Education's 1972–73 survey, found that 26 percent of the women and only 10 percent of the men were unpublished in journals. In a later study by Astin (1984), a comparison of publication rates for women and men from national surveys conducted in 1969, 1972, and 1980 showed that the men outproduced the women in each time period, but that the growth in productivity among academic women was greater than that among men between 1969 and 1980. In a study of 526 men and women scientists in astronomy, biochemistry, chemistry, earth sciences, mathematics, and physics, Jonathan Cole and Zuckerman (1984) found men were more prolific than women, publishing 11.2 papers compared with 6.4 during a 12-year period. Other authors also report gender differences in publications and citations (see, for example, Cole, J. 1979; Hargens, McCann, and Reskin 1978).

The evidence suggests that the correlates of research performance for men and women are not the same, despite early studies that suggested common correlates for both men and women (Folger, Astin, and Bayer 1970). Women respond differently from men to the reinforcement they receive through citations (Cole, J. and Zuckerman 1984). Women may need more encouragement than men to maintain the level of publication they set for themselves early in their careers. The caliber of the Ph.D. department is more important for men's research performance than for women's. Also, women benefit more from employment in a tenure-track position and from postdoctoral fellowships, and they are more influenced by citations than men (Reskin 1978).

Gender, however, is an insignificant correlate of productivity when compared with other correlates (Bernard 1964; Blackburn, Behymer, and Hall, 1978; Cameron and Blackburn 1981; Cole, J. and Zuckerman 1984).When gender appears important (such as in the study by Hargens, McCann, and Reskin 1978), the influence is only indirect because it correlates highly with other variables. Blackburn, Behymer, and Hall (1978) state: "Much of what we see on the surface as sex differences for productivity can be explained by examining the sex differences in variables which most strongly correlate with productivity" (p. 138).

Prestige of Doctoral Program and Mentoring
Graduate programs socialize students to the values and norms of the profession. Brim and Wheeler (1966, p. 83) described this as the "process of movement through the setting," whereby a training program socializes students to enter the faculty ranks; after students assume faculty positions, informed controls and sanctions push them toward activities perceived as valuable (Bess 1978).

This process has interested productivity writers, and studies have explored the relationship between the prestige of the doctoral department and research performance. The studies employ various prestige measures: Long (1978) used the Roose and Anderson (1970) scale; Reskin (1979), the Cartter (1966) scale; and Crane (1965), the Keniston (1959) scale. Studies show that completing a doctorate (used as the terminal degree of study rather than the master's degree) from a prestigious department has short-lived effect on research performance. The effect lasts only through the first six years, possibly through the first decade, after graduation (Long 1978; Reskin 1979). Whether the doctoral department creates an "indelible mark on the student's career," as Caplow and McGee (1958, p. 193) suggested, is questionable. The impact of the department declines over time and is replaced by the influence of the first academic job (Hargens and Hagstrom 1967).

Reskin (1979) attributed the influence of doctoral department on productivity during the first decade to the high-quality training, the resources available, and the eminence of faculty serving on student committees. In addition, she contended that the graduate selection process operates to attract talented students to quality programs. Crane (1965) discussed this process:

Most of the best students are channeled into the best graduate schools and, in turn, the best of these are selected for training by the top scientists. This highly

select group becomes the next generation's most pro-
ductive scientists, most frequently chosen for positions
in major universities (p. 705).

As Crane suggests, top scientists select talented students as mentees. Working with an eminent mentor affects the productivity of the student in the predoctoral phase of training (Reskin 1979) and in the early years after receipt of the doctorate (Long 1978). Close collaboration between student and mentor typically ceases after the degree is granted, but the impact of early publication continues to influence the student's rate of publication for at least three years (Long 1978). Mentors provide superior training and a professional orientation to graduate students, and bright students seek out productive mentors (Reskin 1979). Zuckerman (1977) discussed common mentoring relationships that developed between Nobel laureates and their students.

Neither the prestige of the doctoral department nor graduate student affiliation with an eminent mentor, therefore, strongly affects the long-term productivity of scholars. While Cameron and Blackburn (1981) found that sponsorship variables (e.g., early collaboration with senior faculty) influence performance, the relative influence of sponsorship was minimal. The place of work strongly predicted high research performance. Long (1978) explained away much of the influence of a mentor because of the strong impact of three and six years of the work environment of an institution.

Prestige of Employing Institution
Major universities attract talented graduated students to their positions (Crane 1965). But employment in a prestigious institution shapes and stimulates individual research performance. As Long (1978) pointed out, biochemists attain position because of factors related to graduate education, sponsorship, and postdoctoral study. Once a graduate is employed in a prestigious institution, the correlation between the prestige of the institution and productivity grows larger over time. Then, when the faculty moves, the effects of the prior department and institution dissipate, and the influence of the new department on the scholar increases markedly within five years. Results from Long and McGinnis's (1981) study of biochemists support this

finding. Within three to six years of obtaining a position in a specific context, the biochemist's level of productivity conformed to the characteristics of that context. Compared with citation counts for faculty in research universities, the number of citations to publications of biochemists involved in industrial research, teaching in four-year colleges, or administering a laboratory declined. For those scientists who moved to another institution, Long and McGinnis found that within six years after the move, productivity was largely determined by the context of the new position.

Why prestigious departments or institutions enhance productivity is unclear (Fox 1983). Crane (1965) attributed it to the recruitment of talented graduates by major universities or the visibility and contacts that accrue to faculty in major institutions. Long (1978) reasoned that superior departments may have the prescience to select those individuals who will become productive. Papers submitted by faculty in prestigious departments may appear superior and be more readily accepted for publication. Prestigious departments and institutions tend to be larger and to possess resources and colleagues that facilitate research.

Spending too much or too little work time on research actually may impede performance.

Resources and Assignment

Resources contribute to a productive research career, and high-quality institutions typically have access to money, time for faculty research, competent assistants, stimulating colleagues for faculty, and easy access to information (Allison and Stewart 1974). Allison and Stewart (1974) measured resources as the percentage of work time spent on research, the number of research assistants, and the proportion of respondents who reported that they "always" get the grants they seek (p. 603). From a sample of biologists, mathematicians, physicists, and chemists, they found work time spent on research to be an important predictor of high research performance. During an academic career, the amount of work time spent on research continued to be substantial for productive scholars and declined for less productive ones.

Spending too much or too little work time on research actually may impede performance. Pelz and Andrews (1966) established that the lowest levels of success in journal-article productivity were associated with spending either a very small or a very large proportion of time on research. They found that a mixture of research and nonresearch, such as teaching and administration, facilitated research performance. Knorr et al. (1979) suggested that spending less than 10 percent or more than 80 percent of one's time on research was associated with low research achievement. Productivity peaked when about one-third of a scientist's time was spent on research. The remaining time might be spent on teaching and administration.

Administrative duties may provide the necessary resources that actually enhance performance. Knorr et al. (1979) tested the proposition that scientific productivity was associated with the status or position a scientist held in the formal or informal hierarchy of the organization. They argued that higher position (i.e., administrative position) contributed to productive research because "a scientist's publication capacity is multiplied by the task force he or she supervises and by the project (and other) money to which he or she gains access" (pp. 57–58). Knorr et al. examined this intriguing proposition using a data set of scientists located in academic and industrial organizations. They found that once a scientist attained a supervisory position, manpower resources and project tasks contributed to high research performance.

Colleagues

Productive researchers are those individuals who maintain regular contacts with colleagues, especially research-oriented colleagues (Behymer 1974). Interpersonal contacts, such as visits and telephone conversations with colleagues outside the institution, seem to affect research performance significantly. Pelz and Andrews (1966) found that high research performers contacted a large number of people, spent time making those contacts, and maintained semiweekly or daily contact with colleagues. Braxton (1983) examined the impact of departmental colleagues on individual research productivity by studying the work habits of chemistry and psychology professors in liberal arts colleges. A liberal arts professor who had seldom or never published in the past was likely to publish somewhat more if departmental colleagues were productive scholars than if the colleagues were low research performers. A high research producer, however, was little affected by the publication activity of departmental colleagues.

Finkelstein (1982) explored the impact of colleagues off campus as well as on campus. He examined collegial interaction with departmental colleagues, extradepartmental campus colleagues, and off-campus disciplinary colleagues for faculty in a private university and two liberal arts colleges. He discovered that productive faculty combined strong off-campus collegial functioning with strong departmental interactions and relative insulation from extradepartmental campus colleagues. Thus, he called attention to the importance of both on- and off-campus colleagues in the life of productive scholars.

Colleagues are an important source of information for productive scholars. Parker, Lingwood, and Paisley (1968) explored the relationship between communication behavior and research productivity for "communication researchers" and individuals included in the National Science Foundation's 1966 National Register of Scientific and Technical Personnel. The authors defined communication behavior as "interpersonal contact," including receipt of preprints and unpublished papers; telephone conversations; personal contact, visits, and telephone or correspondence contact with major research facilities; and conversation, correspondence, or unpublished papers as a source of recent useful information. "Impersonal contact" included reading journals, using reprints, maintaining contact with major research facilities, and presenting papers at formal meetings. Results showed interpersonal contacts to be a better predictor of productivity than impersonal contacts. Thirty-one percent of the variance in productivity was accounted for by the predictors in a regression model.

Academic Rank and Tenure

Academic rank and tenure are also related to research productivity according to the literature. For example, faculty who are in the higher professorial ranks have larger publication records than faculty in the lower ranks (Blackburn, Behymer, and Hall 1978). This result is to be expected; however, it may not be as trivial as it seems. The larger question is whether advancement in rank is an incentive to produce scholarly research. Such may be the case; for example, when productivity was compared among faculty with a similar number of years in higher education, those with a higher rank tended to be higher research producers than those with a lower rank (Creswell, Patterson, and Barnes 1984a). Whether academic rank causes high productivity or vice versa is an open question (Wanner, Lewis, and Gregorio 1981). Because of the unclear causal direction between rank and productivity, researchers may need to hold academic rank constant in studies and use it as a controlled or mediating variable.

Whereas academic rank is highly related to productivity, tenure appears to exercise little influence on performance levels. In a study of sociologists, Holley (1977) found a posttenure falloff in research output for faculty, regardless of institutional affiliation. In a study of four departments (physics, chemistry, sociology, and political science), Neumann (1979) discovered little difference in publication rates between tenured and nontenured faculty, though the differences were apparent in distinguished departments. Blackburn, Behymer, and Hall (1978) concluded that few errors will be made in granting tenure to productive faculty. In addition, tenure may not be an incentive to publish.

Early Productivity

Productivity early in a faculty member's career is an excellent predictor of later productivity. One measure of early productivity is the chronological age at the time of first publication. In a study of Ph.D.'s in sociology, Clemente (1973) identified a high negative association between age of first publication and number of articles and books published. Meltzer (1949–50) also established a high negative association between age at time of first publication and a weighted index of publication counts. These studies, along with comments by Manis (1951), suggest that high producers start publishing early in their careers.

A second measure of early publications is the productivity of scholars in the first few years after they receive their doctorate. Lightfield (1971) determined that sociologists who were highly published and cited during the first five years following receipt of their doctorate continued to publish during a second five-year period. For chemists, Reskin (1979) established that early high research performance, measured by the number of articles published during the third, fourth, and fifth years after the Ph.D., was highly predictive of the number of published articles after 10 years (decade publications). She attributed this result to the impact of a high-quality Ph.D. department as well as to such material factors as employment settings and access to resources. Stephen and Jonathan Cole (1967) established that few physicists who start their careers slowly as producers ever become highly productive during their professional life.

One surrogate measure of early productivity can be "prior productivity," defined as the number of publications in the two years prior to collecting data from faculty about their publications (Blackburn, Behymer, and Hall 1978). In a national sample of faculty, Blackburn, Behymer, and Hall (1978) found that two-year performance was an excellent predictor of total career articles, thus confirming that high producers continue to publish throughout their careers.

Preference for Research
Productive researchers are committed to and prefer research to teaching or other activities. Blackburn, Behymer, and Hall (1978) concluded that when the effects of academic discipline and rank were controlled, preference for research emerged as the strongest predictor of total journal-article productivity over a career. Faculty who were intrinsically motivated, successful, and sincerely interested in research were the high performers. In contrast to medium or low performers, these high performers continued to publish throughout their careers, and their interest in research also remained constant.

Creswell, Barnes, and Wendel (1982) identified primary interest in research (as opposed to teaching) as the strongest predictor of journal-article productivity in a battery of 25 correlates. Their correlation matrix also showed a high relationship between interest in research and institutional affiliation ($r = .25$) and weekly hours spent on research ($r = .68$). Thus, individuals who indicated a strong preference for research were employed in institutions that both rewarded research and encouraged it through released time. However, because preference for research correlates positively with other variables, its precise impact on performance is uncertain. Its influence may be indirect. Whether a preference for research causes high performance or high performance causes the preference needs further examination.

Disciplinary Differences

The correlate studies that use the disciplinary affiliation of faculty in the analyses address two concerns: whether research performance differs for faculty from different disciplines, and whether disciplinary affiliation predicts research productivity.

Conclusive evidence shows that faculty research differs among the disciplines. For example, Wanner, Lewis, and Gregorio (1981) compared productivity variables for three disciplinary categories: natural sciences, social sciences, and humanities. They rank-ordered the disciplines from the largest to the smallest output. Natural scientists produced the most journal articles, followed by social scientists and humanities faculty. For book publications, the social scientists were the most prolific publishers, followed by humanities faculty and natural scientists. Thus, the norms regarding productivity emphasize the importance of writing books in the humanities and journal articles in the natural sciences. Biglan (1973) documented this trend with his finding that scholars in the "hard" area (e.g., chemistry) produced more journal articles than scholars in the "soft" area (e.g., accounting), whereas faculty in the "soft" area produced more monographs and books than faculty in the "hard" area.

Though research productivity differs among disciplines, membership in a discipline is not a strong predictor of research performance. In one study, disciplinary membership explains little of the overall variance in journal-article and book productivity when compared with other factors (Creswell, Barnes, and Wendel 1982). Disciplinary membership, though, may exercise an indirect influence on research performance. The causal path may be that research processes and cognitive structures cause differences among disciplines that influence performance. Hargens (1975) found the level of "routinism" differed among 638 mathematicians, chemists, and political scientists. Chemists exhibited a high degree of "routinism" in that they encountered fewer barriers to their progress on research than did mathematicians. Chemists also collaborated more, worked with more graduate students, and were less apt to be distracted from their research than political scientists and mathematicians. In another study, Bayer and Dutton (1977) established different aging and research-performance trends for faculty in seven disciplines. Wanner, Lewis, and Gregorio (1981) confirmed that the number of journals in different disciplines influenced the number of publications for individual faculty. Biglan (1973) showed that membership in a highly codified discipline influences social connectedness (i.e., collaboration). This, in turn, permits greater productivity because research problems can be subdivided with confidence that the results for each part can be reintegrated (Biglan 1973).

Summary and General Observations
Numerous studies examine correlates likely to influence faculty research productivity. No single study incorporates all possible correlates, but major correlates studied include: intelligence test scores, motivation, personality characteristics, stress, age, gender, prestige of doctoral program and mentoring, prestige of employing institution, resources and assignment, colleagues, rank and tenure, early productivity, preference for research, and disciplinary differences.

The studies reviewed suggest several important observations:

First, the predictive power of a correlate is largely a function of the criterion measure of performance. For example, those correlates that influence journal-article productivity differ from those that affect book productivity. Wanner, Lewis, and Gregorio (1981) found that weekly time at research, institutional quality, and number of grants predict the production of journal articles but not books. Creswell, Barnes, and Wendel (1982) established that preference for research predicted journal-article productivity but not book productivity.

Second, evidence suggests that psychological and individual correlates (e.g., intelligence scores) hold less explanatory power regarding performance than sociological and work-environment correlates (e.g., prestige of employing institution) (Blackburn and Havighurst 1979). Psychological measures, however, suffer from imprecise measurement and insufficient tests. Sociological measures, such as preference for research, time spent on research, and early productivity, are extensively discussed in the literature.

Third, a complete explanation for why some faculty are high research producers and others are not is not available.

But multivariate analyses have explained as much as 60 percent of the variance in journal-article productivity (Blackburn, Behymer, and Hall 1978). In multivariate analyses of national faculty data, significant correlates of journal-article and book counts were employment in a high-quality institution, discipline, academic rank, a preference for and time for research, and early prior productivity (Blackburn, Behymer, and Hall 1978; Creswell, Barnes, and Wendel 1982; and Wanner, Lewis, and Gregorio 1981). These correlates are generally consistent with a composite portrait of the productive researcher advanced by Finkelstein (1984, p. 98):

- holds the doctorate;
- is strongly oriented toward research;
- began publishing early, perhaps prior to receipt of the doctorate and received "recognition" for scholarly contributions (Cole, J. and Cole, S. 1973; Reskin, 1977);
- is in close contact with developments in his or her field via interaction with colleagues and keeping abreast of the literature; and
- spends more time in research, less time in teaching, and is not overly committed to administrative chores (although this may vary over institutional prestige strata; see Fulton and Trow 1974).

Fourth, unclear interaction effects and causality cloud the precise relationship between some correlates and productivity. Age, disciplinary membership, and institutional affiliation exercise a mediating influence on research performance. A preference for research may cause high performance as well as result from it. In sum, research performance is a product of a complex set of correlates. Unfortunately, the complete causal model has yet to be specified and solving the "productivity puzzle" eludes researchers (Cole, J. and Zuckerman 1984).

IMPLICATIONS FOR PRACTICE AND FUTURE RESEARCH

Faculty concern for increasing their skill in research and scholarship seems to be particularly acute at this time. This probably reflects both a natural desire on the part of faculty to broaden their professional lives as well as a realistic response to changing pressures within their institutional reward structures (Blackburn et al. 1980, p. 48).

Assuming that faculty seek to enhance their skills in research and scholarship, what are the implications for practice of the literature on research performance (measures, explanations, and correlates)? Any relationship between performance studies and practice is uncharted territory. Though writers have not addressed the implications, two are mapped in this section: the implications of the productivity literature for faculty research development and for the evaluation of faculty research performance. Following this discussion, several themes for future scholarly investigation are addressed.

Faculty Research Development

How do faculty develop as researchers? The most obvious answer is through graduate programs that train them and socialize them to perform research. However, this answer is unsatisfactory because skills learned in graduate school may wane through disuse. Another answer is through a reward system that pressures faculty to publish and write to be promoted and tenured. However, empirical evidence suggests that perceived pressure to publish has no independent effect on research productivity (Behymer 1974). Faculty tend to publish because of inner stimuli rather than external forces (Pelz and Andrews 1966). Faculty may also develop as researchers through self-improvement gained by participation in faculty development activities. But not all faculty can profit equally from development activities. As Fox (1983, p. 229) reported:

Little can be done to affect the least productive, and nothing need be done that could affect the most productive. However, the scientists in the middle who offer a good deal but do not benefit from cumulative advantage may be an effective target for efforts to increase both opportunity and productivity in science.

Any relationship between performance studies and practice is uncharted territory.

The burden for improved performance clearly remains with the faculty, both individually and collectively, though faculty initiatives should be tied to institutional missions (Kirschling 1979).

Faculty development consists of "program activities, practices, and strategies that aim both to maintain and to improve the professional competence of individual faculty" (Mathis 1982, p. 646). Traditionally, faculty development has emphasized instruction and teaching activities. However, the field is in transition from a narrow focus on instructional improvement to a broader purpose, including organizational development and faculty career development (Toombs 1983). Part of faculty career development could be "research development," though writers have not specified the nature of the activities. Blackburn et al. (1980) noted that when faculty were asked about the areas in which they needed professional improvement, improvement in teaching ranked first, but research-oriented activities—manuscript preparation and publication, proposal writing, and computer use—ranked second, third, and fourth in universities and received modest support in liberal arts colleges.

Traditional faculty development activities include some research activities. Among faculty development strategies for research, Gaff (1975) listed sabbatical leaves, travel to meetings of professional associations, and research support. Toombs (1975) argued that the professional development of faculty should include secretarial and technical-aid support, as well as equipment and funds for travel.

The development of faculty as researchers can extend beyond these traditional research activities. Faculty can improve their own research performance—and be assisted by academic administrators—through knowledge of and application of the literature on faculty research performance. The correlates discussed earlier can be organized into ascriptive (givens), individually controlled, and institutionally controlled factors to provide practical strategies to improve faculty research performance (see Table 5). Because ascriptive factors are beyond the control of individuals and organizations, only individual and institutional factors are discussed here.

TABLE 5
ASCRIPTIVE, INDIVIDUALLY CONTROLLED, AND INSTITUTIONALLY CONTROLLED FACTORS INFLUENCING RESEARCH PERFORMANCE

(Givens)
Ascriptive Factors

- Sex of individual (gender)
- Age of a faculty member at a given point in time (chronological age)
- Intelligence, possibly measured by standardized intelligence tests or standardized entrance tests, e.g., GRE, MAT (I.Q. or ability)
- Personality of the individual, e.g., ego-strength, exactness (personality)

Individually Controlled Factors

- Quality and prestige of the doctoral program selected at the pre-career stage (doctoral program)
- Interaction with mentors, sponsors, and influential faculty during the doctoral program (mentor or sponsorship)
- Time—number of years of professional experience—when a faculty member's first manuscript is accepted for publication (age of first publication)
- Publications during the first few years of a professional career—typically within the first five years (early publication)
- Continuous productivity during an academic career (prior productivity)
- Motivation of individual to produce or absence of "hung-up" periods (motivation)
- Extent to which colleagues regionally or nationally are contacted on a regular basis by phone or letter (colleagues)
- Preference for research as opposed to teaching or service that develops through reinforcement processes, e.g., acceptance of manuscripts for publication or citations by colleagues (preference for research)

Institutionally Controlled Factors

- Quality of the institution determined by the quality of faculty hired (prestige of institution)
- Pace at which faculty are advanced in rank (promoted) and tenured in the institution (academic rank, tenure)
- Institutional resources allocated to research, e.g., computer time, research assistants, assignment of faculty time (resources, assignment)
- Values of research ascribed by individuals in the department, college, or institution (colleagues)

Individually controlled factors

Faculty can influence their own performance in several ways.

First, advantages initially accrue to high performers during graduate school. Graduate students in prestigious departments or institutions can gain an initial advantage in establishing a research career by collaborating with distinguished scientists on research projects (Cameron and Blackburn 1981; Crane 1965; Long 1978).

Second, individuals who produce early in their careers become productive researchers throughout their careers (Cole, J. and Cole, S. 1973; Lightfield 1971). One author even suggests that publications should occur within the first five years of receipt of the doctorate (Lightfield 1971). Therefore, faculty should make a concerted effort to publish soon after graduate school. On securing a first academic position, faculty are sometimes diverted from research into teaching and service. Even though the reward system is based heavily on research, course preparations, student advisement, and departmental committees consume large amounts of time. Though these activities are valuable, they detract from work on manuscripts and from the development of the "habit of writing" (Blackburn, Behymer, and Hall 1978). New faculty would do well to establish this "habit" early and begin submitting manuscripts within five years of graduation.

Third, high research producers are individuals who maintain a continuous line of research during their careers. They continue to produce throughout their careers without experiencing a mid-career slump in performance (Creswell, Patterson, and Barnes 1984b). This suggests that a distinct line of inquiry, lasting five or more years, might be initiated by all individuals aspiring to high performance.

Faculty can also expect periods of being "hung-up," periods in which a research theme stalls out temporarily. In these periods, it is important to pursue simultaneous projects because one project may reach an impasse (Hargens 1978).

Fourth, it is also extremely important to maintain research contacts with individuals pursuing similar research within and outside one's employing institution (Braxton 1983; Finkelstein 1982; Parker, Lingwood, and Paisley 1968). Contact should be maintained on a continuous basis through letters, phone calls, and annual conferences. These contacts not only provide encouragement for research ideas but also assist in gaining collaboration opportunities and appointments to journal editorial boards and in achieving a better understanding of the body of literature on a subject.

Fifth, a reinforcement process occurs through publishing manuscripts. Faculty who publish are encouraged to continue publishing (Fox 1983). One cannot overestimate the importance of being cited for worthwhile publications, being contacted for reprints of articles, and being sought out by graduate students who seek to replicate or extend works. The influence of the printed word is powerful, as accomplished researchers can testify. Moreover, publications and citations encourage an individual's preference and orientation to perform research instead of teaching and service. This preference may be further stimulated by the institution through assignments to spend time on research projects and provision of other resources (Allison and Stewart 1974; Knorr et al. 1979).

Institutionally controlled factors

Academic administrators and faculty committees can enhance the research performance of faculty in several ways.

First, graduate students from prestigious doctoral programs are more productive researchers than students from less prestigious programs (Crane 1965). Deans and departmental chairs can seek applicants for positions from prestigious programs by reviewing quality ratings of doctorate-granting departments listed in the five-volume *Assessment of Research-Doctorate Programs in the United States*, published by the Committee on an Assessment of Quality-Related Characteristics of Research-Doctorate Programs in the United States (see Webster 1983). Although some institutions may not have the resources to hire graduates from the best graduate programs, they can attempt to contact graduates from outstanding programs.

Second, obtaining tenure in a department or college does not contribute to improved research productivity (Holley 1977). Thus, no gains are to be made in research performance by tenuring unproductive researchers. On the other hand, academic rank is reliably related to high research performance (Blackburn, Behymer, and Hall 1978). Faculty who are productive researchers seem to be promoted faster than faculty who are less productive. Therefore, for personnel committees to hold all faculty to the same time-in-rank guidelines makes little sense, especially for productive researchers.

Third, to be high research performers, faculty need time assigned to their faculty load for research (Allison and Stewart 1974). Oddly enough, this simple point is often overlooked by faculty and administrators. The time assigned need not be excessive. Knorr et al. (1979) maintained that the time should not exceed 80 percent or be less than 20 percent; somewhere in the range of 40 percent is probably ideal. Adequate computer time, research assistants, and secretarial services are other valuable resources in a productive research career.

Ingalls (1982) discussed a research program to increase faculty productivity in one small Canadian university. The program included the following elements:

- the creation of an office of research administration and the appointment of a director of research and publications;
- the creation of a presidential committee to make recommendations on research policy and the allocation of internally funded research grants;
- the implementation of hiring policies intended to recruit and retain faculty with either a proven record of research productivity or the potential to develop a research program;
- the allocation of funds from the university's operating budget to provide seed money to support the research of promising scholars;
- the establishment of a faculty research seminar;
- the allocation of faculty travel funds on a priority basis to those attending conferences to present their research findings; and
- the creation of a program of sabbatical leave grants (pp. 60–61).

Fourth, the attitude and atmosphere of a department or college are important in stimulating high productivity among faculty (McKeachie 1983). Becker (1977, p. 21) commented: "Sincerely expressed interest in what the researchers are doing, sympathy for their problems, and sincere praise for what they feel are breakthroughs they have made are bound to encourage further productive activity."

Appreciative departmental chairs and administrators who respect the research performance of faculty provide an environment that is stimulating for researchers. Departmental chairs can be role models for high research performance, and senior colleagues can collaborate with or assist junior faculty in research. Departmental goals and objectives can be oriented toward research; faculty can share outstanding research achievements with colleagues in departmental meetings; and lists of publications can be developed and updated annually for departments and colleges. Such efforts attest to a supportive environment in which individuals place value on research.

Faculty Evaluation and Research Productivity
How does the literature on research productivity assist chairs, deans, university-wide administrators, and personnel committees responsible for the evaluation of faculty performance? Before answering this question, a brief review of the literature on faculty evaluation is helpful.

Faculty are evaluated to improve their performance; to assist personnel decisions, such as promotion, tenure, and salary determinations; to guide students in the selection of courses and instructors; and to provide data to individuals and organizations operating off campus (Seldin 1980). Various assessment tools are used to measure faculty performance, such as self-appraisal forms, peer-appraisal forms, personnel-committee forms, and forms that are used university-wide. Evaluation of research performance is a major component of faculty evaluation not only in universities but also in state colleges, and more recently, it has assumed new importance in liberal arts colleges (Seldin 1984b).

The literature on research productivity can inform faculty evaluations in several important ways.

First, a major finding from the productivity literature is that research performance varies by discipline and type of institution (e.g., Bayer and Dutton 1977; Blackburn, Behymer, and Hall 1978). Thus, it comes as no surprise that disciplines and types of institutions (see, e.g., the Carnegie Commission on Higher Education 1973) differ in the kinds of information used in making promotion, tenure, and salary decisions. In a study of the kinds of information used by chairs to evaluate faculty research performance, Centra (1977) found three important types of information: the number of articles published in quality journals, the number of books of which the faculty member is the sole or senior author, and the quality of the faculty member's research publications as determined by peers at the institution. However, the relative weight given to the kinds of information differs by academic field and by institution. For example, in research universities, faculty research performance is judged by the number of grants obtained; in the social sciences, by articles in quality journals, internal and external peer evaluations, and appointments as journal editors; in the humanities, books; and in the natural sciences, a combination of grants, journal publications, and citations. Patterns also differed for faculty in doctorate-granting and comprehensive universities and colleges.

The practical implications of these findings are important for personnel committees and university administrators who review faculty credentials from several departments and disciplines. The importance lies in the need to use disciplinary, even departmental, standards for assessment rather than university-wide procedures. As Roskens (1983, p. 292) commented,

> *those who advocate subject area standards point out that, when a scholar's work is evaluated, those who conduct the evaluation should recognize the value of the scholar's activities, since scholarly activities differ depending upon the subject area. Consequently, any interpretation of faculty evaluation policies should reflect these differences, and subject area, not single university-wide or single discipline perspectives, should be used to reflect that scholarly achievement. . . .*

Assessing the standards applicable at the lowest level in an organization is probably a wise procedure for evaluators. The kinds of information used to assess productivity and research performance vary from campus to campus. And single, statewide standards of performance cannot be applied uniformly without a recognition of the diversity of institutional measures.

A second finding from the research literature is that academics' attitudes and performance differ at various stages in their research careers (e.g., Baldwin 1979; Fulton and Trow 1974). For example, mean ratings of the following decline during a career: comfort with research scholarship; research competence and involvement as a major professional strength; and pleasure at the opportunities for research, scholarship, and growth and development (Baldwin and Blackburn 1981). With this information as a guide, those responsible for faculty evaluation should emphasize the "developmental" aspect of the academic career, acknowledging the changes and fluctuations in the attitudes and interests of faculty (Baldwin and Blackburn 1981). Such an emphasis will help college administrators and individual professors to understand the attitudes that are dominant at different times in a career.

Departmental or college reward systems based heavily on research performance for senior faculty overlook the strong teaching orientation that pervades the near-retirement phase of a career. To expect a senior professor who has never published to start publishing late in his or her career creates an impossible task for that teacher and a frustrating experience for faculty evaluators.

Third, the following are useful generalizations for personnel committees:

The importance lies in the need to use disciplinary, even departmental, standards for assessment rather than university-wide procedures.

- Since research performance is a multidimensional concept, personnel committees should use several measures of performance (Yuker, 1978).
- When publication and citation counts are used, personnel committees should recognize their strengths and weaknesses. For example, when publication counts are used, it is helpful to assess the quality of the journal or book. Jauch and Glueck (1975), for example, recommended that the best approach is the use of simple counts of articles modified by weighting the count by a quality-journal index. This index can be prepared by faculty most familiar with the quality journals (e.g., departmental faculty), though Jauch and Glueck realized that obtaining faculty agreement on the quality journals might be difficult.
- Personnel committees might consider a broad definition of research and identify levels of acceptable performance. Centra (1976), Jauch and Glueck (1975), and Seldin (1984a) provided a starting point, and their measures can be aggregated into quantitative, qualitative, peer-judgment, and eminence categories, as shown in Table 6. Other measures may also be considered because of disciplinary orientations, such as

TABLE 6
MEASURES OF RESEARCH IN FACULTY EVALUATION STUDIES

Jauch and Glueck (1975)   **Centra (1976); Seldin (1984a)**

Quantitative Measures

Number of papers, books, and technical reports published; number of papers presented at professional meetings

Publications in all professional journals; papers at professional meetings; books, sole or senior author; books, junior author or editor; monographs or chapters in books; grants or funding received; unpublished papers or reports

Qualitative Measures

Index of journal quality; citations to published materials; success rate of proposals for research support

Articles in quality journals; citations to published materials

Peer Judgments

Peer evaluations; self-evaluations

Peers at institution; peers at other institutions; self-evaluation; departmental chairs; deans

Eminence Measures

Referee or editor of scientific journal; recognition-honors and awards from profession; officer of national professional association; invited papers and guest lectures; number of dissertations supervised

Referee or editor of scientific journal; honors or awards from profession

patents, new methods developed for industry, and creative productions. Personnel committees must first understand research as it is defined in units and then identify acceptable levels of high performance.

- The lines between scholarship and teaching or service, for example, are becoming increasingly blurred (Braxton and Toombs 1982; Pellino, Blackburn and Boberg 1984). Personnel committees must keep in mind that some faculty view research, teaching, and service as ''scholarship'' activities. Thus, even faculty who do not publish may still perceive their work to be scholarly (Pellino, Blackburn and Boberg 1984).
- Finally, personnel committees can issue research performance guidelines for new faculty, chairs, and deans that are consistent with the mission of the college and institution. As Seldin (1980) recommended, personnel

committees should make known their preferences and how they weigh research. Personnel committees can assign weights to different research products (e.g., grants, books, articles, and so forth). Becker (1977) reminded us that faculty are responsible for the choice of products; once researchers develop their plans, the leadership should support such plans through collegial assistance and help elaborate those plans into refined research proposals consistent with organizational directions.

Research Agendas

This synthesis of the literature raises questions for future scholarly investigation.

The measures of research productivity in empirical investigations are excessively narrow. Beyond publication and citation counts, researchers employ few measures. Yet, the criteria used to assess research performance vary widely from one type of institution to another. **Empirical studies should examine broader measures of research (e.g., grants obtained, patents, creative projects, and others) and determine the correlates that have positive predictive influence.**

An interdisciplinary approach is needed to study faculty research performance. The conceptual basis for this recommendation is not drawn simply from the sociology of science or from psychology, but also from adult and occupational development theories and the history and evolution of science. As Fox (1983) commented, the challenge for productivity studies lies in the capacity of scholars to combine perspectives. This means that scholars must cross strict disciplinary lines to study and explain high performance. Though as much as 60 percent of the variance in productivity is explained in some studies, understanding high scholarly performance is far from complete.

More studies should address the correlates of the work environment. Because colleagues, resources, time for research, and even a supportive environment are crucial for high performance, subtle socialization processes are also operative, as well as specific reward systems of institutions (such as how merit pay is tied to research performance in a given institution). Unfortunately, knowledge about the exact impact of the work environment on individual research performance is limited. Researchers might consider using academic rank, discipline, institutional affiliation, and perhaps even career stages (i.e., years of professional experience in higher education) as control variables in a predictive model and examine closely the significant correlates of productivity that are related to the work environment of the scholar.

More attention should be given to the relationship between faculty career stages and research performance. No clear consensus exists as to whether productivity increases, remains stable, fluctuates, or declines as faculty age. Perhaps all age curves are valid given certain dependent measures, and research is needed to establish the measures and conditions under which one curve rather than another operates. Also, attaching curves to changes in personal life and occupation is an elusive but necessary area for future research. An interdisciplinary team drawn from developmental psychology, psychology, and sociology should probe this area.

Most studies of research productivity are devoid of practical suggestions for personnel employed in institutions of higher education. One noticeable lack is faculty development. Current and past faculty development studies emphasize the development of teaching skills to the exclusion of development of research skills. **Studies should relate the development of faculty as researchers to career or developmental stages.** For example, what assistance does the assistant professor with five years experience need to prepare for promotion and tenure review? How do the activities of full professors with 10 years left until retirement relate to research development activities? Given the increased emphasis on research, questions and activities bearing on faculty research development should be widely discussed in the coming decade in order to make our understanding of faculty research efforts more precise.

Summary
The research performance literature can inform faculty and academic administrators about strategies for developing faculty as researchers and for evaluating faculty research performance. For faculty development, in addition to traditional sabbatical leaves, attendance at professional association meetings, and research monies, the performance liter-

ature offers several strategies for improved faculty productivity. Faculty can select outstanding graduate programs for their training, begin publishing soon after achieving the doctorate, maintain a continuous level of research throughout their careers, keep in continuous contact with other scholars working on similar research projects, and establish a preference for research (e.g., set priorities for research activities) in their work schedule. Administrators and faculty committees can reinforce and stimulate faculty research efforts by employing graduates of research-oriented institutions, granting promotions and tenure to faculty who are productive researchers, providing faculty with time and resources to conduct scholarly work, and creating an attitude and atmosphere in a department or college that values research.

In the faculty evaluation process, those who evaluate faculty should realize that research performance varies by discipline and that university- or college-wide standards are inappropriate to assess productivity. Research performance also varies with the stages of a faculty career. Evaluation committees might consider performance levels in conjunction with the academic rank and years of experience of faculty. Committees can also recognize that several measures of research performance should be assessed and acknowledge the strengths and limitations of publication and citation counts. When publication counts are used to evaluate performance, those counts can be supplemented by a qualitative index of the publications. Regardless of the measures used, faculty and administrators should recognize that the meaning of scholarship and research is changing in higher education, and new faculty, deans, and evaluation committees must be informed of changing administrative practices in various units of the institution.

Finally, the literature on scholarly productivity suggests several future research themes. Future scholarly studies should include multiple measures of research productivity as dependent variables; utilize an interdisciplinary approach to conceptual explanations; examine the importance of the work environment on productivity holding constant such factors as academic rank, institution, discipline, and career stage; and suggest practical implications of the results for faculty and administrators in higher education.

REFERENCES

The ERIC Clearinghouse on Higher Education abstracts and indexes the current literature on higher education for the National Institute of Education's monthly bibliographic journal *Resources in Education*. Most of these publications are available through the ERIC Document Reproduction Service (EDRS). For publications cited in this bibliography that are available from EDRS, ordering number and price are included. Readers who wish to order a publication should write to the ERIC Document Reproduction Service, P.O. Box 190, Arlington, Virginia 22210. When ordering, please specify the document number. Documents are available as noted in microfiche (MF) and paper copy (PC). Because prices are subject to change, it is advisable to check the latest issue of *Resources in Education* for current cost based on the number of pages in the publication.

Allison, Paul D. May 1980. "Inequality and Scientific Productivity." *Social Studies of Science* 10: 163–179.

Allison, Paul D., and Stewart, John A. August 1974. "Productivity Differences Among Scientists: Evidence for Accumulative Advantage." *American Sociological Review* 39: 596–606.

Andrews, Frank M., ed. 1979. *Scientific Productivity: The Effectiveness of Research Groups in Six Countries*. Cambridge: Cambridge University Press.

Astin, Helen. 1969. *The Woman Doctorate in America*. New York: The Russell Sage Foundation.

———1978. "Factors Affecting Women's Scholarly Productivity." In *The Higher Education of Women: Essays in Honor of Rosemary Park,* edited by Helen Astin and Werner Z. Hirsch. New York: Praeger Publishers.

———1984. "Academic Scholarship and Its Rewards." In *Advances in Motivation and Achievement,* vol. 2, edited by Marjorie W. Steinkamp and Martin L. Maehr. Greenwich, Conn.: JAI Press.

Babchuk, Nicholas, and Bates, Alan P. May 1962. "Professor or Producer: The Two Faces of Academic Man." *Social Forces* 40: 341–348.

Baldwin, Roger G. 1979. "Adult and Career Development: What Are the Implications for Faculty?" In *Current Issues in Higher Education, No. 2, 1979*. Washington D.C.: American Association for Higher Education. ED 193 998. 44 pp. MF–$0.97; PC not available EDRS.

Baldwin, Roger G., and Blackburn, Robert T. November–December 1981. "The Academic Career as a Developmental Process." *Journal of Higher Education* 52(6): 598–614.

Bayer, Alan E. June 1970. "College and University Faculty: A Statistical Description." *ACE Research Reports* 5: 1–48. ED 042 425. 46 pp. MF–$0.97; PC–$5.34.

——1973. "Teaching Faculty in Academe: 1972–73." *ACE Research Reports* 8: 1–68. ED 080 517. 65 pp. MF–$0.97; PC–$7.14.

Bayer, Alan E., and Dutton, Jeffrey E. May–June 1977. "Career Age and Research-Professional Activities of Academic Scientists." *Journal of Higher Education* 48: 259–282.

Bayer, Alan E., and Folger, John. 1966. "Some Correlates of a Citation Measure of Productivity in Science." *Sociology of Education* 39: 381–390.

Bean, John. 1982. "A Causal Model of Faculty Research Productivity." Paper presented at the annual meeting of the American Educational Research Association, March, New York, New York. ED 216 661. 33 pp. MF–$0.97; PC–$5.34.

Becker, H. 1977. "Productivity Issues in Research: The Personal Perspective of One Researcher." In *Proceedings of a National Conference on Productivity and Effectiveness in Educational Research and Development*. Philadelphia, Pa.: Research for Better Schools, Inc. ED 151 971. 76 pp. MF–$0.97; PC–$9.36.

Behymer, Charles A. 1974. "Institutional and Personal Correlates of Faculty Productivity." Ph.D. dissertation, University of Michigan.

Bernard, Jessie. 1964. *Academic Women*. University Park, Pa.: Pennsylvania State University Press.

Bess, James. 1978. "Anticipatory Socialization of Graduate Students." *Research in Higher Education* 3: 289–317.

Biglan, Anthony, June 1973. "The Characteristics of Subject Matter in Different Academic Areas." *Journal of Applied Psychology* 57(3): 195–203.

Blackburn, Robert T.; Behymer, Charles E.; and Hall, David E. April 1978. "Research Notes: Correlates of Faculty Publications." *Sociology of Education* 51: 132–141.

Blackburn, Robert T., and Havighurst, Robert J. September 1979. "Career Patterns of U.S. Male Academic Social Scientists." *Higher Education* 8(5): 553–572.

Blackburn, Robert T.; Pellino, Glenn R.; Boberg, Alice; and O'Connell, Coleman. 1980. "Are Instructional Improvement Programs Off-Target?" In *Current Issues in Higher Education, No. 1, 1980*. Washington D.C.: American Association for Higher Education. ED 194 004. 63 pp. MF–$0.97; PC not available EDRS.

Blume, S. S., and Sinclair, R. February 1973. "Chemists in British Universities: A Study of the Reward System in Science." *American Sociological Review* 38: 126–138.

Braxton, John M. Winter 1983. "Department Colleagues and Individual Faculty Publication Productivity." *The Review of Higher Education* 6(2): 115–128.

Braxton, John M., and Toombs, William. 1982. "Faculty Uses of Doctoral Training: Consideration of a Technique for the Differentiation of Scholarly Effort from Research Activity." *Research in Higher Education* 16(3): 265–282.

Brim, Orville G., and Wheeler, Stanton. 1966. *Socialization After Childhood: Two Essays.* New York: John Wiley & Sons.

Cameron, Susan W., and Blackburn, Robert T. July–August 1981. "Sponsorship and Academic Career Success." *Journal of Higher Education* 52(4): 369–377.

Caplow, Theodore, and McGee, Reece J. 1958. *The Academic Marketplace.* Garden City, New York: Anchor Books.

Carnegie Commission on Higher Education. 1973. *A Classification of Institutions of Higher Education.* Berkeley, Calif.: Carnegie Commission on Higher Education. ED 217 742. 150 pp. MF–$0.97; PC–$12.96.

Carnegie Council on Policy Studies in Higher Education. 1980. *Three Thousand Futures: The Next Twenty Years for Higher Education.* San Francisco: Jossey-Bass. ED 183 076. 175 pp. MF–$0.97; PC not available EDRS.

Cartter, Alan M. 1966. *An Assessment of Quality in Graduate Education.* Washington D.C.: American Council on Education.

Cattell, Raymond B. 1963. "The Personality and Motivation of the Researcher from Measurements of Contemporaries and from Biography." In *Scientific Creativity: Its Recognition and Development,* edited by Calvin W. Taylor and Frank Barron. New York: John Wiley & Sons.

Centra, John A. November 1976. "Faculty Development Practices in U.S. Colleges and Universities." Princeton, N.J.: Educational Testing Service. ED 141 382. 96 pp. MF–$0.97; PC–$9.36.

———. 1977. *How Universities Evaluate Faculty Performance: A Survey of Department Heads.* GRE Board Research Report GREB No. 75-5bR. Princeton, N.J.: Graduate Record Examinations Program, Educational Testing Service. ED 157 445. 26 pp. MF–$0.97; PC not available EDRS.

Clark, Kenneth E. 1957. *America's Psychologists: A Survey of a Growing Profession.* Washington D.C.: American Psychological Association.

Clemente, Frank. November 1972. "Measuring Sociological Productivity: A Review and a Proposal." *The American Sociologist* 7:7–8.

———. September 1973. "Early Career Determinants of Research Productivity." *American Journal of Sociology* 79(2):

409–419.

Cole, Jonathan R. 1979. *Fair Science*. New York: The Free Press.

Cole, Jonathan R., and Cole, Stephen. 1973. *Social Stratification in Science*. Chicago: The University of Chicago Press.

Cole, Jonathan R., and Zuckerman, Harriet. 1984. "The Productivity Puzzle: Persistence and Change in Patterns of Publication of Men and Women Scientists." In *Advances in Motivation and Achievement*, Vol. 2, edited by Marjorie W. Steinkamp and Martin L. Maehr. Greenwich, Conn.: JAI Press.

Cole, Stephen. January 1979. "Age and Scientific Performance." *American Journal of Sociology* 84: 958–977.

Cole, Stephen, and Cole, Jonathan R. June 1967. "Scientific Output Recognition: A Study in the Operation of the Reward System in Science." *American Sociological Review* 32: 377–390.

Collins, W. Andrew. March 1971. "Identifying and Fostering Productive Researchers: An Occasional Paper from ERIC at Stanford." Palo Alto, Calif.: Stanford University ERIC Clearinghouse on Educational Media and Technology. ED 047 538. 33 pp. MF–$0.97; PC–$5.34.

Cox, Lawrence M. 1980. "Scientific Productivity: A Critical Test of Several Hypotheses." Ph.D. dissertation, Southern Illinois University.

Crane, Diane. October 1965. "Scientists at Major and Minor Universities: A Study of Productivity and Recognition." *American Sociological Review* 30: 699–714.

Creswell, John W.; Barnes, Michael W.; and Wendel, Fred. 1982. "Correlates of Faculty Research Productivity." Paper presented at the annual meeting of the American Educational Research Association, March, New York, New York.

Creswell, John W.; Patterson, Robert A.; and Barnes, Michael W. 1984a. "Enhancing Faculty Research Productivity." Paper presented at the meeting of the Association for the Study of Higher Education, March, Chicago, Illinois.

———. 1984b. "Low and High Research Producers: A Career Perspective." Paper presented at the annual meeting of the American Educational Research Association, April, New Orleans, Louisiana.

Finkelstein, Martin J. 1982. "Faculty Colleagueship Patterns and Research Productivity." Paper presented at the annual meeting of the American Educational Research Association, March, New York, New York. ED 216 633. 42 pp. MF–$0.97; PC–$5.34.

———. 1984. *The American Academic Profession*. Columbus: Ohio State University Press.

Folger, John K.; Astin, Helen S.; and Bayer, Alan E. 1970.

Human Resources and Higher Education: Staff Report of the Commission on Human Resources and Advanced Education. New York: The Russell Sage Foundation.

Fox, Mary Frank. May 1983. "Publication Productivity Among Scientists." *Social Studies of Science* 13(2): 285–305.

Fulton, Oliver, and Trow, Martin. Winter 1974. "Research Activity in American Higher Education." *Sociology of Education* 47: 29–73.

Gaff, Jerry. 1975. *Toward Faculty Renewal*. San Francisco: Jossey-Bass.

Garfield, Eugene. 1979. *Citation Indexing—Its Theory and Application in Science, Technology, and Humanities*. New York: John Wiley & Sons.

Gaston, Jerry. 1978. *The Reward System in British and American Science*. New York: John Wiley & Sons.

Glenn, Norval D., and Villemez, Wayne. August 1970. "The Productivity of Sociologists at 45 American Universities." *American Sociologist* 5: 244–251.

Gmelch, Walter H.; Wilke, Phyllis Kay; and Lovrich, Nicholas P. 1984. "Sources of Stress in Academe: Factoral Dimensions of Faculty Stress." Paper presented at the annual meeting of the American Educational Research Association, April, New Orleans, Louisiana.

Hagstrom, Warren O. 1965. *The Scientific Community*. New York: Basic Books.

Hammel, Eugene. 1980. "Report of the Task Force on Faculty Renewal." Mimeographed. Berkeley, Calif.: Berkeley Population Research, University of California.

Hargens, Lowell L. 1975. *Patterns of Scientific Research: A Comparative Analysis of Research in Three Scientific Fields*. The Arnold and Caroline Rose Monograph Series. Washington, D.C.: American Sociological Association.

————. February 1978. "Relations Between Work Habits, Research Technologies, and Eminence in Science." *Sociology of Work and Occupations* 5: 97–112.

Hargens, Lowell L., and Hagstrom, Warren O. Winter 1967. "Sponsored and Contest Mobility of American Academic Scientists." *Sociology of Education* 40(1): 24–38.

Hargens, Lowell L.; McCann, James C.; and Reskin, Barbara F. September 1978. "Productivity and Reproductivity: Fertility and Professional Achievement Among Research Scientists." *Social Forces* 57(1): 154–163.

Hicks, Loretta P. December–January 1978–79. "Abundance or Richness in Output." *Community and Junior College Journal* 50(4): 10–13.

Holley, John W. 1977. "Tenure and Research Productivity."

Research in Higher Education 6: 181–192.

Horowitz, Stephen M.; Blackburn, Robert T.; and Edington, Dee W. 1984. "Some Correlates of Stress with Health and Work/Life Satisfaction for University Faculty and Administrators." Paper presented at the annual meeting of the Association for the Study of Higher Education, March, Chicago, Illinois.

Hunter, Deborah E., and Kuh, George D. 1984. "A Profile of Prolific Scholars in Higher Education." Paper presented at the annual meeting of the American Educational Research Association, April, New Orleans, Louisiana.

Ingalls, Wayne B. 1982. "Increasing Research Productivity in Small Universities: A Case Study." *The Canadian Journal of Higher Education* 12(3): 59–64.

Jauch, Lawrence R., and Glueck, William F. September 1975. "Evaluation of University Professors' Research Performance." *Management Science* 22(1): 66–75.

Kaplan, Norman. 1964. "Sociology of Science." In *Handbook of Modern Sociology,* edited by Robert E. Faris. Chicago: Rand McNally.

Keniston, Hayward. 1959. *Graduate Education and Research in the Arts and Sciences at the University of Pennsylvania*. Philadelphia: University of Pennsylvania Press.

Kirschling, Wayne, ed. 1978. *Evaluating Faculty Performance and Vitality*. San Francisco: Jossey-Bass.

———. 1979. "Conceptual Problems and Issues in Academic Labor Productivity." In *Academic Rewards in Higher Education,* edited by Darrell R. Lewis and William E. Becker, Jr. Cambridge, Mass.: Ballinger.

Knorr, Karin D.; Mittermeir, Roland; Aichholzer, Georg; and Waller, Georg. 1979. "Individual Publication Productivity as a Social Position Effect in Academic and Industrial Research Units." In *Scientific Productivity: The Effectiveness of Research Groups in Six Countries,* edited by Frank M. Andrews. Cambridge: Cambridge University Press.

Kroc, Richard J. 1983. "Measuring Scholarly Productivity." Ph.D. dissertation, University of Colorado at Boulder.

———. June–July 1984. "Using Citation Analysis to Assess Scholarly Productivity." *Educational Researcher* 13(6): 17–22.

Kuhn, Thomas S. 1970. *The Structure of Scientific Revolutions*. Chicago: University of Chicago Press.

Ladd, Everett C., Jr. 1979. "The Work Experience of American College Professors: Some Data and an Argument." In *Current Issues in Higher Education, No. 2, 1979*. Washington D.C.: American Association for Higher Education. ED 193 998. 44 pp. MF–$0.97; PC not available EDRS.

Ladd, Everett C., Jr., and Lipset, Seymour M. 1978. *Technical*

Report, 1977 Survey of the American Professoriate. Storrs: Social Science Data Center, University of Connecticut.

Lazarsfeld, Paul F., and Thielens, Wagner, Jr. 1958. *The Academic Mind.* Glencoe, Ill.: The Free Press.

Lehman, Harvey C. 1953. *Age and Achievement.* Princeton: Princeton University Press.

Lightfield, E. Timothy. May 1971. "Output and Recognition of Sociologists." *The American Sociologist* 6: 128–133.

Lindsey, Duncan. 1978. *The Scientific Publication System in Social Science.* San Francisco: Jossey-Bass.

———. May 1980. "Production and Citation Measures in the Sociology of Science: The Problem of Multiple Authorship." *Social Studies of Science* 10: 145–162.

Lodahl, Janice B., and Gordon, Gerald. February 1972. "The Structure of Scientific Fields and the Functioning of University Graduate Departments." *American Sociological Review* 37: 57–72.

Long, John S. December 1978. "Productivity and Academic Position in the Scientific Career." *American Sociological Review* 43: 889–908.

Long, John S., and McGinnis, Robert. August 1981. "Organizational Context and Scientific Productivity." *American Sociological Review* 46: 422–442.

Lotka, Alfred J. June 1926. "The Frequency Distribution of Scientific Productivity." *Journal of the Washington Academy of Sciences* 16(12): 317–322.

MacRoberts, Michael H., and MacRoberts, Barbara R. August 1982. "A Re-Evaluation of Lotka's Law of Scientific Productivity." *Social Studies of Science* 12: 443–450.

Manis, Jerome G. March 1951. "Some Academic Influences Upon Publication Productivity." *Social Forces* 29: 269–272.

Manning, Charles W., and Romney, Leonard C. 1973. *Faculty Activity Analysis: Procedures Manual.* Technical Report No. 44. Boulder, Colo.: National Center for Higher Education Management Systems. ED 084 998. 146 pp. MF–$0.97; PC–$12.96.

Mathis, B. Claude. 1982. "Faculty Development." In *Encyclopedia on Educational Research,* edited by H. E. Mitzel. New York: The Free Press.

McKeachie, Wilbert J. December 1983. "Faculty as a Renewable Resource." In *College Faculty: Versatile Human Resources in a Period of Constraint,* edited by Roger G. Baldwin and Robert T. Blackburn. New Directions for Institutional Research No. 40. San Francisco: Jossey-Bass.

McPherson, J. H. 1963. "A Proposal for Establishing Ultimate Criteria for Measuring Creative Output." In *Scientific Creativity: Its Recognition and Development,* edited by Calvin W.

Faculty Research Performance

Taylor and Frank Barron. New York: John Wiley & Sons.

Meisinger, Richard J.; Purves, Ralph A.; and Schmidtlein, Frank A. Winter 1975. "Productivity from an Interorganizational Perspective." In *Measuring and Increasing Academic Productivity,* edited by Robert W. Walhaus. New Directions for Institutional Research, Vol. II, No. 4. San Francisco: Jossey-Bass.

Meltzer, Bernard. July 1949–50. "The Productivity of Social Scientists." *American Journal of Sociology* 55: 25–29.

Merton, Robert, ed. 1973. *The Sociology of Science: Theoretical and Empirical Investigations*. Chicago: The University of Chicago Press.

Merton, Robert K., and Gaston, Jerry. 1977. *The Sociology of Science in Europe*. Carbondale: Southern Illinois University Press.

Neumann, Yoram. May 1979. "Research Productivity of Tenured and Nontenured Faculty in U.S. Universities: A Comparative Study of Four Fields and Policy Implications." *The Journal of Educational Administration* 17: 92–101.

Over, Ray. September 1982. "Does Research Productivity Decline with Age?" *Higher Education* 11(5): 511–520.

Parker, Edwin B.; Lingwood, David A.; and Paisley, William J. July 1968. *Communication and Research Productivity in an Interdisciplinary Behavioral Science Research Area*. Stanford University, California Institute for Communication Research. Springfield, Va.: National Technical Information Service.

Pellino, Glenn R.; Blackburn, Robert T.; and Boberg, Alice. 1984. "The Dimensions of Academic Scholarship: Faculty and Administrator Views." *Research in Higher Education* 20(1): 103–115.

Pelz, Donald C., and Andrews, Frank M. 1966. *Scientists in Organizations*. New York: John Wiley & Sons.

Price, Derek J. De Solla. 1963. *Little Science, Big Science*. New York: Columbia University Press.

Reskin, Barbara F. June 1977. "Scientific Productivity and the Reward Structure of Science." *American Sociological Review* 42: 491–504.

———. 1978. "Scientific Productivity, Sex, and Location in the Institution of Science." *American Journal of Sociology* 83: 1235–1243.

———. July 1979. "Academic Sponsorship and Scientists' Careers." *Sociology of Education* 52: 129–146.

———. 1980. "Age and Scientific Productivity: A Critical Review." In *The Demand for New Faculty in Science and Engineering. Proceedings of the Workshop of Specialists in Forecasts of Demand for Scientists and Engineers, 1979,* edited by Michael S. McPherson. Washington, D.C.: Commission on

Human Resources, National Research Council, National Academy of Sciences. ED 193 067. 257 pp. MF–$0.97; PC–$20.89.

Roe, Anne. 1953. *The Making of a Scientist*. New York: Dodd, Mead.

———. May 1972. "Patterns in Productivity of Scientists." *Science* 176: 940–941.

Roose, Kenneth D., and Anderson, Charles J. 1970. *A Rating of Graduate Programs*. Washington, D.C.: American Council on Education.

Roskens, Ronald W. 1983. "Implications of Biglan Model Research for the Process of Faculty Advancement." *Research in Higher Education* 18(3): 285–297.

Seldin, Peter. 1980. *Successful Faculty Evaluation Programs*. Crugers, New York: Coventry Press.

———. 1984a. *Changing Practices in Faculty Evaluation*. San Francisco: Jossey-Bass.

———. 1984b. "Faculty Evaluation: Surveying Policy and Practices." *Change* 16(3): 28–33.

Smith, Richard, and Fiedler, Fred E. Summer 1971. "The Measurement of Scholarly Work: A Critical Review of the Literature." *Educational Record* 52: 225–232.

Storer, Norman. 1973. "Introduction." In *The Sociology of Science: Theoretical and Empirical Investigations,* edited by Robert K. Merton. Chicago: The University of Chicago Press.

Taylor, Calvin W., and Barron, Frank. 1963. *Scientific Creativity: Its Recognition and Development*. New York: John Wiley & Sons.

Taylor, Calvin W., and Ellison, Robert L. March 1967. "Biographical Predictors of Scientific Performance." *Science* 155 (3765): 1075–1080.

Toombs, William. November–December 1975. "A Three-Dimensional View of Faculty Development." *Journal of Higher Education* 46(6): 701–717.

———. 1983. "Faculty Development: The Institutional Side." In *College Faculty: Versatile Human Resources in a Period of Constraint,* edited by Roger G. Baldwin and Robert T. Blackburn. New Directions for Institutional Research No. 40. San Francisco: Jossey-Bass.

Wallhaus, Robert A., ed. 1975. *Measuring and Increasing Academic Productivity*. New Directions for Institutional Research No. 8. San Francisco: Jossey-Bass.

Wanner, Richard A.; Lewis, Lionel S.; and Gregorio, David I. October 1981. "Research Productivity in Academia: A Comparative Study of the Sciences, Social Sciences, and Humanities." *Sociology of Education* 54: 238–253.

Webster, David S. May–June 1983. "America's Highest Ranked

Graduate Schools, 1925–1982." *Change* 15(4): 14–24.

Whitely, Richard D. 1977. "The Sociology of Scientific Work and the History of Scientific Developments." In *Perspectives in the Sociology of Science,* edited by Stuart S. Blume. New York: John Wiley & Sons.

Wilson, Logan. 1942. *The Academic Man.* New York: Oxford University Press.

Yuker, Harold E. April 1978. "Measuring Faculty Productivity." In *The Uniqueness of Collective Bargaining in Higher Education. Proceedings, Sixth Annual Conference,* edited by A. Levenstein. New York: National Center for the Study of Collective Bargaining in Higher Education, City University of New York. ED 168 449. 111 pp. MF–$0.97; PC not available EDRS.

Ziman, J. M. 1968. *Public Knowledge: An Essay Concerning the Social Dimension of Science.* Cambridge: The University Press.

Zuckerman, Harriet. Spring 1970. "Stratification in American Science." *Sociological Inquiry* 40: 235–257.

———. 1977. *Scientific Elite: Nobel Laureates in the United States.* New York: The Free Press.

Zuckerman, Harriet, and Merton, Robert K. 1973. "Age, Aging and Age Structure in Science." In *Sociology of Science,* edited by Robert K. Merton. Chicago: The University of Chicago Press.

INDEX

A

Ability, 29
Academic Man, The, 2
Academic rank, 27, 31, 39–40, 49
Access to information, 37
Administrative duties, 38
Administrators: role in enhancing research, 49, 50
Affiliation, 36–38, 44
Age curve, 32
Age factor, 18, 31–33, 40
American Men of Science, 15
American Council on Education, 8, 15, 34
American Journal of Sociology, 10
American Sociological Review, 10
Arts and Humanities Citation Index, 11
Ascriptive factors in research performance, 47
Assessment of Research-Doctorate Programs in the United States, 49

B

Bivariate design (correlate studies), 27
Books/monographs vs. journal articles, 42

C

Career stages, 52–53, 56
Carnegie Commission, 15
Carnegie Corporation of New York, 3
Causal model (correlate studies), 27, 42
Chemical Abstracts, 10
Citation counts, 7–9, 11–14, 29, 37, 53
Collaboration, 43, 47, 48, 51
Colleagues: effect of, 38–39
Committee on an Assessment of Quality-Related Characteristics of Research-Doctorate Programs in the United States, 49
Committees, personnel (see Personnel policy)
Communication behavior, 39, 48
Composite portrait of productive researcher, 44
Continuity of research theme, 48
Correlates of productivity, 27–44
Creativity, 30
Cumulative advantage: as explanation for research productivity, 18–19, 25, 28

D

Data bases of faculty resarch, 22–23
Definition of research, 53

Departmental attitudes, 50
Disciplinary differences, 42–43, 51–52
Disciplinary norms, 21–25, 28
Disciplinary research variances, 24
Doctoral program effect, 35–36, 49
Doctorate: value of, 44

E

Early publishing effect, 36, 40–41, 44, 48
Eminence measures of performance, 8
Employer prestige, 36–37
Environmental effects, 43, 50–51, 55–56
ERIC database, 8, 14
Evaluation standards, 52

F

Faculty development, 45–51, 56–57
Faculty evaluation, 51–55, 57
Faculty recruitment, 50
Funds for research, 50

G

Gender factor, 17–18, 33–35
Graduate student selection, 35–36, 49
Grants obtained, as measure of productivity, 8, 37

H

Habit of writing, 21, 48
Halo effect, 14
Hierarchical position of researcher, 38
Hiring policy, 50
Humanities: productivity norms, 42

I

"Impersonal contacts," 39
Individually controlled factors in research performance, 47–49
Innate talent, 16, 25
Institutionally controlled factors in research performance, 47, 49–51
Intelligence test scores, 29
Interest in research, 40
Interpersonal contact, 38–39

J

Journal articles published, 16, 42–43
Journal Citation Report, 11

L

Liberal arts colleges, 38–39, 46

M

Macro-organizational model (correlate research), 27
Market worth of faculty, 13
Mathematical distribution of performance, 15
"Matthew effect," 19
Measures of research, 7–9, 54, 55
Mentoring factor, 35–36
Motivation for research, 1, 29–30, 34, 41, 45

N

National Aeronautics and Space Administration, 30
National Center for Higher Education Management Systems, 4
National Institutes of Health, 4
National Medal of Science, 11
National Register of Scientific and Technical Personnel, 39
National Science Foundation, 39
National surveys of faculty research, 22–23
Natural sciences: productivity norms, 42
Nobel laureates: study of, 3, 15, 36
Nobel prizes, 11
Norms, 21–25

O

Office of research administration, 50

P

Paradigm structure, 23–24
Patents, 8, 55
Peer ratings, 7, 9, 13–14
Performance variability, 25
Personality traits, 17, 30–31
Personnel policy
        evaluation, 53–55
        hiring, 50
        tenùre decisions, 49
Posttenure falloff in output, 40
Predictor variables, 27–44
Preference for research, 41
Prestige of department/program, 29, 34–36, 47, 49
Prestige of employing institution, 36–37
"Prior productivity," 41
Productivity (see also Research performance)
        correlates of, 27–44

definition, 3
factors, 2
faculty development: individually controlled, 47–49
faculty development: institutionally controlled, 49–51
faculty evaluation, 51–55
future research themes, 57
ideal program for, 50
studies of, 22–23
Prolific scholars, 30
Psychological explanations of productivity, 16–18, 27, 28
Publication counts, 7–11, 14, 29, 40, 44, 53
Publication quality, 11
Publication rate, 3, 15, 34, 36
Publication type, 42, 51–52

Q
Quality indicators, 11

R
Ratings (see Peer ratings)
Recognition, 20–21, 31
Reinforcement as explanation of research performance, 19–21, 28, 49
Reputation, 13
Research and development atmosphere, 3
Research agendas, 55–56
Research assistants, 37
"Research development" (see Faculty development)
Research performance (see also Productivity)
ascriptive factors, 47
conceptual explanations, 15–25
correlates of, 27–44
disciplinary differences, 42–43, 51–52
evaluation of, 52–53
individually controlled factors, 47–49
institutionally controlled factors, 47, 49–51
levels, 1–2
measures, 7–9, 54, 55
studies, 2–3, 22–23, 27–28
theoretical base for study, 3–4
Research productivity (see Productivity)
Research program elements, 50
Researchers
composite description of, 44
faculty view as, 1
promotion of productive, 49
Resources, 37–38, 50–51

Reward systems, 3, 31, 40, 45, 53
Role models (see also Mentoring factor), 51
"Routinism," 42

S

Sabbatical leaves, 50
"Sacred spark" concept, 17, 25
Scholarly journals, 8
"Scholarship" definition, 54
Science Citation Index, 7, 11, 14
Scientist productivity, 30
Self-reported data, 10
Seminars: faculty research, 50
Senior faculty, 53, 56
Sex differences (see Gender factor)
Social-position model (correlate research), 27
Social Science Citation Index, 11, 14
Social sciences: productivity norms, 42
Social structure of institutions, 3
Socialization of graduate students, 35, 45
Sociological correlates of productivity, 43
Sociology of science, 3
Sponsorship variables, 36
Standards for assessment, 52
Straight publication counts, 8
Strategies for individual success, 47–48
Stress, 31
Structure of Scientific Revolutions, The, 23
Support staff/services, 37, 46, 50
Survey of the American Professoriate, 15

T

Tenure, 39–40, 49
Thorndike Award, 11
Time spent on research, 37–38, 50
Travel funds, 50

W

Weighted publication counts, 8, 10, 11
Women's productivity, 18, 34
Work environment correlates of productivity, 43, 50–51, 55–56
Workload, 50

ASHE-ERIC HIGHER EDUCATION REPORTS

Starting in 1983, the Association for the Study of Higher Education assumed cosponsorship of the Higher Education Reports with the ERIC Clearinghouse on Higher Education. For the previous 11 years, ERIC and the American Association for Higher Education prepared and published the reports.

Each report is the definitive analysis of a tough higher education problem, based on a thorough research of pertinent literature and institutional experiences. Report topics, identified by a national survey, are written by noted practitioners and scholars with prepublication manuscript reviews by experts.

Eight monographs (10 monographs before 1985) in the ASHE-ERIC Higher Education Report series are published each year, available individually or by subscription. Subscription to eight issues is $55 regular; $40 for members of AERA, AAHE and AIR: $35 for members of ASHE. (Add $7.50 outside the United States.)

Prices for single copies, including 4th class postage and handling, are $7.50 regular and $6.00 for members of AERA, AAHE, AIR, and ASHE ($6.50 regular and $5.00 for members for reports published before 1983). If faster 1st class postage is desired for U.S. and Canadian orders, add $.75 for each publication ordered: overseas, add $4.50. For VISA and MasterCard payments, include card number, expiration date, and signature. Orders under $25 must be prepaid. Bulk discounts are available on orders of 15 or more reports (not applicable to subscriptions). Order from the Publications Department, Association for the Study of Higher Education, One Dupont Circle, Suite 630, Washington, D.C. 20036, (202/296-2597. Write for a publication list of all the Higher Education Reports available.

1985 Higher Education Reports

1. Flexibility in Academic Staffing: Effective Policies and Practices
   Kenneth P. Mortimer, Marque Bagshaw, and Andrew T. Masland

2. Associations in Action: The Washington, D.C., Higher Education Community
   Harland G. Bloland

3. And on the Seventh Day: Faculty Consulting and Supplemental Income
   Carol M. Boyer and Darrell R. Lewis

4. Faculty Research Performance: Lessons from the Sciences and the Social Sciences
   John W. Creswell

1984 Higher Education Reports

1. Adult Learning: State Policies and Institutional Practices
   K. Patricia Cross and Anne-Marie McCartan

2. Student Stress: Effects and Solutions
   Neal A. Whitmar, David C. Spendlove, and Claire H. Clark

3. Part-time Faculty: Higher Education at a Crossroads
   Judith M. Gappa

---

4. Sex Discrimination Law in Higher Education: The Lessons of the Past Decade
   J. Ralph Lindgren, Patti T. Ota, Perry A. Zirkel, and Nan Van Gieson

5. Faculty Freedoms and Institutional Accountability: Interactions and Conflicts
   Steven G. Olswang and Barbara A. Lee

6. The High-Technology Connection: Academic Industrial Cooperation for Economic Growth
   Lynn G. Johnson

7. Employee Educational Programs: Implications for Industry and Higher Education
   Suzanne W. Morse

8. Academic Libraries: The Changing Knowledge Centers of Colleges and Universities
   Barbara B. Moran

9. Futures Research and the Strategic Planning Process: Implications for Higher Education
   James L. Morrison, William L. Renfro, and Wayne I. Boucher

10. Faculty Workload: Research, Theory, and Interpretation
    Harold E. Yuker

1983 Higher Education Reports

1. The Path to Excellence: Quality Assurance in Higher Education
   Laurence R. Marcus, Anita O. Leone, and Edward D. Goldberg

2. Faculty Recruitment, Retention, and Fair Employment: Obligations and Opportunities
   John S. Waggaman

3. Meeting the Challenges: Developing Faculty Careers
   Michael C. T. Brookes and Katherine L. German

4. Raising Academic Standards: A Guide to Learning Improvement
   Ruth Talbott Keimig

5. Serving Learners at a Distance: A Guide to Program Practices
   Charles E. Feasley

6. Competence, Admissions, and Articulation: Returning to the Basics in Higher Education
   Jean L. Preer

7. Public Service in Higher Education: Practices and Priorities
   Patricia H. Crosson

8. Academic Employment and Retrenchment: Judicial Review and Administrative Action
   Robert M. Hendrickson and Barbara A. Lee

9. Burnout: The New Academic Disease
   Winifred Albizu Meléndez and Rafael M. de Guzmán

10. Academic Workplace: New Demands, Heightened Tensions
    Ann E. Austin and Zelda F. Gamson

Yes, I want to receive the other 7 reports in the 1985 ASHE-ERIC Higher Education Report series at the special discount price. I have just bought Report No. ___ at $7.50. Please deduct this amount from the price of my subscription.

Type	Subscription	This issue	TOTAL
Regular	$55.00	−$7.50	$47.50
AERA, AIR, AAHE member	$40.00	−$7.50	$32.50
ASHE member	$35.00	−$7.50	$27.50

". . . A valuable series, especially for reviewing and revising academic programs. These reports can save us all from pitfalls and frustrations."

Mark H. Curtis, former President
Association of American Colleges

Dear Librarian,

I have just finished reading one of the 1985 ASHE-ERIC Higher Education Reports (ISSN 0884-0040). I found it outstanding and strongly recommend that our institution subscribe to the series. At $55.00 for 8 issues, it is a bargain.

Signed,

Name _____

Title _____

Association for the Study of Higher Education
The George Washington University
One Dupont Circle, Suite 630, Dept. 51
Washington, D.C. 20036
Phone: (202) 296-2597

FROM: _____

_____

_____

_____

Association for the Study of Higher Education
Attention: Subscription Department
One Dupont Circle, Suite 630
Washington, DC 20036

FROM: _____

_____

_____

_____

ATTN: Serial Acquisitions Dept.
The Library

_____

_____

_____